PARANORMAL
HAMPSHIRE

PARANORMAL
HAMPSHIRE

DAVID SCANLAN

AMBERLEY

First published 2009

Amberley Publishing Plc
Cirencester Road, Chalford,
Stroud, Gloucestershire, GL6 8PE

www.amberley-books.com

British Library Cataloguing in Publication Data.
A catalogue record for this book is available from the British Library.

ISBN 978 1 84868 257 3

Typesetting and origination by Amberley Publishing
Printed in Great Britain

This book is dedicated to my family.

For the love and support they have all shown me over the years and for putting up with me when I drop everything and go shooting out in the middle of the night to investigate yet another haunting.

CONTENTS

FOREWORD

As a Patron of the Hampshire Ghost Club and a writer and researcher of ghost sightings on the Isle of Wight for more than thirty years myself, I firmly believe there can never be too many well-researched and intelligent books on this most fascinating and enigmatic subject of ghosts and the paranormal.

It is a pleasure when a serious investigator of the paranormal finds a really rational book providing genuine facts and a sensible attitude. Although this is his first book, David Scanlan is, without doubt, set to become the new authority on ghosts and ghostly activity in and around Hampshire.

Although other paranormal experts, including Peter Underwood, have written of sightings, stories of ghosts and hauntings here, David has taken a fresh look at this most haunted county.

Combining his experience as a paranormal researcher with his hands-on, practical experience of ghost hunting and a meticulous approach to the investigations, he brings a no-nonsense attitude to this journey of discovery into hidden worlds.

Historically, we know that ghosts have been talked and written about for thousands of years. Are ghosts real? Who can say, for common sense and simple logic can explain most supposed 'hauntings'. But not all. And it is that small but significant number of extraordinary happenings which defy explanation.

As the noted psychic expert Hans Holzer wrote, "Throughout the centuries, the sceptical, the scientific and the credulous have attempted to solve the mystery of ghosts and hauntings. There are theories but no proofs as to why things happen. But that the incidence of such happenings exceeds the laws of probability and that their number establishes that there is something to investigate, is beyond dispute."

Gay Baldwin
www.ghostisland.com

INTRODUCTION

Back in 2001 I founded the Hampshire Ghost Club, whose aims are to scientifically investigate claims of ghostly encounters experienced by members of the public. The club has met with some considerable success and we have visited many places in Hampshire, and indeed many parts of the United Kingdom, that can claim a haunted heritage and spooky goings on, so it is not surprising that during this journey of discovery into the paranormal I have come across many places that have never been referenced in other literature. Therefore, this book contains many previously unpublished encounters with the supernatural and raises awareness of many never before heard of haunted venues.

The historic county of Hampshire is probably one of the most haunted counties in the entire United Kingdom yet most of the literature surrounding its hauntings, although excellently communicated and well researched, is somewhat repetitive and limited in some circumstances.

With the writing of this book I hope I may have helped rectify this problem as this work not only contains many of the more famous sites in Hampshire but also has numerous haunted houses, castles, stately homes, abbeys, churches, museums and many other venues that have never previously had their hauntings recorded in a book of this nature.

I have attempted to cover as many sites as possible, many of them being open to members of the public, whilst writing this book and if I have omitted any haunts that you feel should have been included then please do accept my apologies and feel free to contact me so I can update future editions.

I would like to take this opportunity to thank everyone who has been involved in the writing of this book. From the staff members at the many haunted sites I have visited, especially those at the Beaulieu estate whose help was invaluable in the writing of the stories associated with their properties, through to my family, friends and team members of the Hampshire Ghost Club whose input and support has been a great source of inspiration and enthusiasm, and finally the biggest thank you must go to you, the reader, without whom this book would not have been possible.

How to use this book

When I sat down to work out a format of content and design for this book it was apparent from an early stage that the best possible layout was to make it an easy to read style of book.

With this in mind I decided to structure the book around an easy to follow A–Z guide, this means that finding the story you are particularly interested in is simple to locate. There is no need for an index as everything is listed in an A–Z format and this allows you to pick up and put down the book as and when required. This is particularly useful when researching specific locations in general but it is also possible to read the book cover to cover.

A GAZETTEER OF HAMPSHIRE HAUNTINGS

ALL SAINTS CHURCH, CRONDALL

If you should happen to be in the small north east Hampshire village of Crondall then be sure to take a short meandering walk around the old Norman churchyard of All Saints as this walk may well herald your own paranormal experience.

During the English Civil war, 1642–1651, the forces loyal to the parliamentarian cause used the church as an improvised defence and when you consider its location, near to the town of Farnham, it is not surprising to discover that the occasional scuffle took place.

The result of one of these scuffles has somehow been left behind and numerous people over the years have encountered the ghosts of those slaughtered in battle. Phantom soldiers have been reported moving around the churchyard of All Saints but the most awe inspiring of its ghosts must be ghostly roundhead soldier seen riding his horse, dressed in full battle armour, up through the avenue of lime trees and vanishing into thin air.

APPULDURCOMBE HOUSE, ISLE OF WIGHT

Appuldurcombe House was once one of the great estates of the Isle of Wight and it's said that the lands of Appuldurcombe and Knighton Gorges, another famous haunted house on the island, were linked by the families who owned them.

Appuldurcombe is referred to as a calendar house as it has 365 windows and 52 rooms, a window for every day of the year and a room for every week of the year. Legends about the house abound and many of these are probably nothing more than urban legends that have lost all control of restraint. However there are a few stories that tend to stick out as having some sense of plausibility, for instance. People claim to have witnessed a ghostly horse drawn carriage that makes no noise, unpleasant smells emanating from a cupboard in the gift shop, a small figure seen drifting from the gate down to the house but when the figure is pursued no one is there, door handles turn on their own and both individuals and groups of monks have been witnessed.

Long term custodian Dennis Cooper who was a firm skeptic when it came to the paranormal was somewhat disgruntled when he was instructed to escort a medium around the house in an attempt to discover if the house was haunted. Dennis had an experience which made him rethink his theories on the paranormal. Mr. Cooper was ascending a staircase in the house when he had the feeling that someone had passed him on the stairs, but when he looked around he could see no one but noticed the flickering of a candle on a wall. The problem here was that candles were not used in the house at that time. Monks are often seen at the house. In 1901 a group of Benedictine monks used the house while nearby Quarr Abbey was being prepared for them and the wraiths of these monks seem to linger on.

During my research into Appuldurcombe house I came across the story that pages in the visitors book apparently turn on their own but when I spoke to the current owner he claims that no guest book exists....or one that he knows of.

During my time as a paranormal investigator I have visited hundreds of haunted venues but none have affected me in the same way that Appuldurcombe house did. I am not psychic in the least bit but the intense and aggressive feeling I felt from the house will not see me rushing back to visit this venue.

BASING HOUSE, BASINGSTOKE

Old Basing was once the capital of England and therefore it is an area steeped in history and ghostly tales.

Basing House was the seat of the Marquis of Winchester, William Paulet, and his home was ranked as the largest private house in England boasting an amazing 380 rooms and standing 5 storeys high. Today it is nothing more than a ruin thanks to the efforts of Sir Oliver Cromwell, Colonel John Dalbier and the 800 parliamentarian troops who laid siege to the house in 1645.

At the end of the siege the great house was no more, Cromwell's troops were permitted to remove what they wished from the house and made off with approximately £10 million pounds worth of goods and valuables. Despite the house being a ruin and the troops all long gone there are some soldiers here that still refuse to leave their posts at Basing House.

Visitors to the site have reported seeing figures dressed in Royalist costumes, one of them being incredibly tall. Excavations at the site revealed a make shift graveyard where the remains of some of the siege victims now rest, surprisingly one of these graves contained the body of a man over 7 foot tall. Perhaps it is the spirit of this dead soldier that still haunts his beloved Basing.

BEAULIEU ABBEY, BEAULIEU, NEW FOREST

The very founding of Beaulieu Abbey in 1204 is deeply rooted in a paranormal legend.

King John, the monarch of England from 1199 to 1216, was very harsh in his treatment of monks and once stated that his men should not pay any heed if they trampled any monk under hoof of horse. Much of this dislike of monastic orders primarily comes from the fact that they petitioned the King for tax relief, something he took great offence too. Following this statement King John had a very vivid nightmare that would change his outlook on the monks and even make him fear for what would become of his soul when he departed this mortal life for the next plane of existence.

As he slept one night the King's nightmare began....he dreamt of being beaten by a group of monks and upon waking realised his body ached from the impact of the monk's batons, and desperate to make amends he granted land to a group of Cistercian monks from Citeaux, France. The monks arrived in 1204 and construction of Beaulieu Abbey began. It is the ghostly monks that lived, worked, prayed and died at the abbey that haunt its 800-year-old ruins. Many people claim to have witnessed white and brown clad figures drifting amongst the abbey ruins, as well as the lanes and fields of the estate.

Four boys in 1954 claimed to have witnessed a small rowing boat, occupied by five monks, come ashore at Beaulieu River whilst they were taking shelter in a small boat house during a night time fishing trip that had been cut short due to bad weather. The monks moored their small vessel on the river bank, disembarked and started to make their way towards the abbey entrance before vanishing into thin air and leaving the four young boys in a rather perplexed and confused state.

The Domus Conversorum, formally the lay brothers dormitory and now a hotbed of supernatural activity.

In the 1960s a former nurse decided to visit the abbey ruins. When she exited the Domus Conversorum, the original lay brothers dormitory and refectory, she was met with the view of the peaceful and serene cloisters. Upon scanning the cloisters she noted a man, dressed in monk's apparel, sitting in a niche reading a scroll. The nurse tried, somewhat in vain, to find a rational explanation for her encounter but she was at a loss to discover one.

In 1964 the famous British actress Margaret Rutherford was at Beaulieu for the filming of a short documentary titled 'The Stately Ghosts of England'. During the filming of this show the actress claims to have also witnessed a ghostly monk sitting in the cloisters, having a quiet read to himself, before promptly vanishing. Continuing on with our stage and screen encounters we come to an experience that was had by a member of a TV crew whilst filming a short film called 'Wonderful Beaulieu'. The cameraman was stood upon a wall in the cloisters, now commonly believed to have been the area where the choir monks dormitory once stood, when a spectral hand lurched forward and apparently attempted to push him off the wall in what would have been a very nasty fall.

One of the estate's most interesting and colourful characters has to be that of the Reverend Robert Frazer Powles. Reverend Powles was the last independent parish priest of Beaulieu Parish Church, the building being previously used in monastic times as the dining room for the choir monks.

The Cloisters of Beaulieu Abbey. It is here that a day visitor witnessed the apparition of a monk sitting quietly reading a scroll.

Reverend Powles claimed to have had many an interesting encounter during his time here. He said that he saw, knew and talked to many of the abbey's ghostly monks and even held a special midnight mass for his spectral friends every Christmas eve. Many people may consider these stories as just that, just stories made up by the ailing mind of an elderly priest, but the Montagu family have always said that Powles, affectionately known to the Montagu children as Daddy Powles, was always of sound mind and not prone to fits of fantasy.

Beaulieu Parish Church. It is here that a former priest claims to have held special services for the ghosts of the abbey's long dead monks.

Miss Aimee Cheshire is also another character in Beaulieu's rich tapestry of hauntings. Miss Cheshire used to occupy a small flat that stood on the first floor of the Domus Conversorum. She also claims to have seen and spoken too many of the phantom monks during her occupancy here. Some of the information she was told by the monks even went into a book she wrote, and the book was sent to an abbot at a monastery in Dijon, France. He was that astounded by the information contained within its pages that he actually came to visit Miss Cheshire to enquire where she had obtained such extraordinary information. I wonder how he took the news that the facts in her book had been relayed to her by a deceased monk?

Beaulieu Abbey is also renowned for its auditory phenomena. The sound of Gregorian chanting, which has been reported by many people over the years and most interestingly by Mrs. Elizabeth Varley, who was even able to recreate the music she had heard, have been reported drifting across the estate. It is said that the monastic chanting usually heralds the death of a villager. The first director of the Motor Museum at Beaulieu, Mr. Michael Sedgwick, claims to have heard the sounds of a ghostly funeral procession and subsequent burial outside his cottage window, a rather disturbing experience considering that later research indicated that the former monks once had their graveyard located in the exact same area.

In October 2007 I was invited to the estate to give a series of lectures and tours about the ghosts of Beaulieu. During one of the breaks I happened to talk to one of the estate's many gardeners who had worked in the grounds for over ten years, he went on to ridicule the stories and after some lively debate I returned to my lectures. The following day the gardener tracked me down and said for the first time in his career at Beaulieu he had encountered something he could not explain. Whilst cutting and pruning the hedges surrounding the abbey's ruined hospital he had noticed the sudden and unexplainable smell of sandalwood. The gardener stated to me that there was nothing in the grounds that could have caused the smell, and what he found even more perplexing was the fact that the scent came and went on a number of occasions in a short space of time. He said that the occurrence had baffled him so much that he decided to pack up and continue pruning the hedges the following day. In October 2008 I met the same gardener who revealed that he had had another encounter, this time whilst working in the Victorian gardens. "I was just working away when someone blew in my ear" he told me.

In addition to the numerous stories I have been told about and researched I too have had my own personal experiences whilst visiting the abbey. Many a time have I been privy to hearing disembodied voices, footsteps, the jangle of keys and of course fleeting glimpses of white clad monks and dark shrouded figures. On an investigation I was conducting on Hallowe'en 2008 a member of my investigation team, Jane Bourne, snapped a most interesting and unusual photograph. The image she obtained apparently shows a humanoid figure with its hands clasped, as if in prayer.

The strange, possibly spectral figure, standing in the cloisters of Beaulieu Abbey on 31 October 2008.

The ghost of a lady dressed in a blue dress has also been witnessed crossing the cloisters and heading towards the Montagu family vault. It is believed this spirit is that of Countess Isabella, a former family member who very nearly lost her family inheritance, but these days she is more commonly reported walking the rooms of the private apartments in Palace House.

BOLDRE CHURCH, NEAR LYMINGTON

Boldre Church, near Lymington in the New Forest, is a Norman church and is first mentioned in texts as early as 1100AD.

Closer inspection of the church's fabric reveals that three Saracen stones have been incorporated into the church's structure. This has led historians and archaeologists to theorise that religious practice on the site has been performed since around 2000BC.

Although rather small the church is home to some spectacular ghosts. Witnesses have seen soldiers entering the church but there is some speculation as to their origins. Some say the soldiers are dressed in battledress of the Norman conquerors, others say their dress resembles that of the Crusaders.

A one Mr. Alexander once had a startling encounter with no less than two prominent ghosts. Whilst at the church, around dusk time, Mr. Alexander witnessed two archers dressed in medieval tunics, their bows resting by their sides, kneeling at the altar in solemn prayer.

Boldre Church near Lymington in the New Forest. The scene of a spectral encounter with two medieval archers.

BRADBEERS DEPARTMENT STORE, ROMSEY

In the town centre of Romsey, just behind Barclays Bank which was once the town's Corn Exchange can be found the department store of Bradbeers.

Bradbeers is a very popular shop with many of the town's local residents nipping in to to purchase everything from perfumes to furniture. During the building's early history the shop was a tavern known as the Dolphin Inn. There is a plaque on the exterior wall confirming to this fact, and it is probably from the building's use as a tavern that the ghost that haunts here is accustomed too.

The apparition of a lady in white, some say blue, has been seen drifting around the older parts of the building. She says nothing when addressed and doesn't even acknowledge the living who now use the building. Perhaps she is some kind of recording that has become embedded into the very fabric of the building and is sadly destined to walk here for eternity.

Bradbeers Department Store in Romsey where fashion, furniture and its resident ghost live happily side by side.

BRAISHFIELD VILLAGE, NEAR ROMSEY

If you happen to be wandering the roads and lanes in the village of Braishfield keep an eye out for an elderly woman in Edwardian dress. The legend in the village is that a wealthy, elderly woman who once lived here, decided to bury her fortune in order to keep it safe.

After doing so the lady became ill and died. Witnesses report seeing the ghostly lady walking around the village, pausing at the gates of cottages and stopping underneath tress. Perhaps she is looking for her lost fortune or maybe, if you meet her, she may just guide you to untold wealth.

BRAMSHILL HOUSE, BRAMSHILL

The rather impressive Jacobean mansion that is Bramshill House is haunted by no less than eleven ghosts, and that's a conservative estimate considering how much phenomena has been sighted over the years.

The ghosts that haunt Bramshill House are as varied as they possibly can be and include spooks from the Stuart period of history right through to the twentieth century. The wraith of a classic haunted house, a white lady has been seen, as well as also a ghostly family consisting of a man, woman and a small boy. The boy is rarely seen although people claim to know of his presence by the sounds of crying.

Over the many years I have been researching and investigating ghosts I have come across many different types of ghosts from numerous periods of history but one of the strangest spectres I have ever heard about haunts Bramshill.

He is known to many as the Green Man but his real name is, or more rather aptly was, Henry Cope. It appears that Mr. Cope had a very strange affection for the colour green, so much so in fact that he only wore green clothes, ate only green vegetables and even decorated his home with green furniture. People who have had an encounter with the Green Man state that he is visible only from the knees up; he appears to have no lower legs.

Investigators researching the ghosts of Bramshill House have theorised this is because Mr. Cope could not obtain green boots and therefore wore a pair of black boots instead. My personal opinion on this facet of his haunting is that the ground level on which the ghost now walks upon is somewhat higher than it once was, therefore to us it appears Henry has no legs, whereas he may just simply be walking upon the ground that his physical body once trod upon.

Henry Cope finally met his end when he committed suicide, on his second attempt, at Brighton beach in East Sussex.

Like many other stately homes of England, Bramshill also has its own version of the Mistletoe Bride legend. A young lady married her sweetheart, around Christmas time, and as part of the jolly japes and high spirits of the celebrations it was decided that a game of hide and seek was in order.

The young bride found a large chest to hide in; she climbed inside, closed the lid and was then unable to free herself from the self locking chest. Her remains were found 50 years later by a housemaid when she opened the chest and came face to face with a skeleton dressed in a wedding gown clutching a sprig of mistletoe. The chest that the poor bride's body was found in is proudly displayed in the hallway of Bramshill House and many people over the years, especially security guards working in the House in the dead of night, have reported seeing the ghost of a young lady dressed in a white dress hanging around the area of the chest, and also in the area of the long gallery. It has also been claimed that this apparition also haunts some of the bedrooms and a past resident stated that on frequent occasions she awoke in the middle of the night to witness this apparition. She is often accompanied in her spectral travels by a sudden decrease in temperature and by also a strong, sweet smelling floral perfume.

The ghost of an old man with a long white beard has been reported peering out of one of the house's many windows and in some cases people claim to have witnessed him leaning over the chest that spirited away the life of the mistletoe bride. Could he be connected to her in some way?

George Abbot, Archbishop of Canterbury from 1611 till 1633, is at the very centre, and indeed is the cause, of our next ghost. In 1622, when the house was owned by Lord Zouche, Bishop Abbot was out hunting when the bolt from his crossbow missed the stag he was taking aim at and struck a keeper, Peter Hawkins, killing him. Abbot's enemies tried to have him removed from the post of Archbishop, claiming that this murder disqualified him from his post, but King James I backed his archbishop and Abbot kept the role. History records that George Abbot was intensely upset over this accident and paid penance once a week for the rest of his life; little did he know that his actions on that fateful day would have eternal repercussions.

There is a tree in the grounds of Bramshill House, an oak tree, known as Keeper's Oak which is where the accident of 1622 occurred and it is here that the ghost of a keeper has been seen.

Anyone for tennis? People have reported seeing a young man moving through the reception hall and passing into a wall, a wall now but once formerly a door in years gone by. They have said that the man is dressed as if going to play a game of tennis. Research into this ghost highlighted a possible identity for him as the son of a former owner who was killed when he fell from a train in the 1930s.

BREAMORE HOUSE, FORDINGBRIDGE

A haunted object is always an interesting curiosity to discover and none more so than the cursed portrait of Mrs. William Dodington that hangs in Breamore House near Fordingbridge in the New Forest.

The construction of Breamore House was completed in 1583 for the Dodington family but passed to the ownership of the Hulse family in 1748; the Hulse family still owns the house to this day and the Breamore House website, www.breamorehouse.com, claims "it is still very much a family home".

When Sir Edward Hulse purchased the house in 1748 he also bought its resident ghost and the haunted portrait of Lady Dodington. The Dodington family was one that appears to have been plagued with misfortune as both murder and suicide occurred in their family history.

First the untimely suicide of William Dodington in 1600 occurred when he jumped from the battlements of St. Sepulchres Steeple in London. His reason for the suicide appears to have been in response to a landownership dispute and in his suicide letter he stated:

John Bulkeley and his fellows by perjury have brought me to this.
Surely after they had thus slandered me, everyday that I lived was to me an hundred deaths, which caused me to choose to die with Infamy, than to live with Infamy and Torment.

But the family's sadness did not end here. In 1629 the grandson of the ill fated William Dodington, Henry Dodington, murdered his own mother and it is her ghost that haunts the blue bedroom to this very day. However, she is rarely seen, which is probably for the best as bearing witness to this apparition is meant to indicate the death of the current owner of Breamore House.

Back to the haunted portrait. One of the conditions of sale when the Hulse family purchased Breamore House was that the portrait of Mrs. Dodington would always hang in the Great Hall and it does to this very day. Touching the portrait is meant to herald the death of the perpetrator on the same day, and despite the portrait's horrifying reputation two people in years gone by have dared to push their luck to the very limit.

One of these was a gentleman who was suffering from depression and wanted to end his life, he was unsuccessful and survived but the second culprit was not so lucky. A member of staff on the estate decided to one day give the portrait a bit of a spruce up and dust it, later that day he fell from a roof whilst fitting a TV ariel and died.

Was the portrait of Mrs. Dodington responsible or was it just an unfortunate twist of fate?

In closing this story I will take the time to mention the estates Mizmaze. The maze has its origins in the medieval period and was the centre of punishment for nearby monks who has committed misdemeanors. The monks were made to crawl around the maze in search for the maze's centre, which doesn't sound too bad until you consider that they did their punishment on bare knees crawling through the rough chalk.

It is claimed that you can still hear the sounds of their monastic moans and groans as they go about their painful penance.

BUCKLER'S HARD, BEAULIEU, NEW FOREST

This former eighteenth-century ship building village, owned and operated by the Beaulieu Estate, is famous for the construction of many ships throughout its history. It is particularly noted for the construction of the battleships *Agamemnon*, *Euryalus* and *Swiftsure* that fought at the Battle of Trafalgar in 1805 under the watchful gaze of Admiral Lord Horatio Nelson.

The ghost that has been witnessed at Buckler's Hard is a somewhat confusing apparition. One would expect a ghostly presence at the Hard to be that of a boat builder or a sailor but the ghost that haunts here is that of a young boy. Another unusual twist in this story is that the ghost is not seen in an old building standing on the site but in the recently built museum. No one knows who he is or why this boy haunts the museum and only time, research and investigation will hopefully shed some light onto the ghost and its reasons for haunting such a place.

An aerial photograph of the haunted village of Buckler's Hard, near Beaulieu, in the New Forest. © Photo supplied with kind permission of Lord Montagu of Beaulieu.

B3078 NEAR BROOK

In May 1924 three young people on their way home had a most extraordinary encounter, not once but three times!

Before the time the motor car was both popular and more financially available to people, many folk used the trusty old bicycle to get around on. Indeed many people would cycle some considerable distances that most people of the current era would faint at the thought of.

One of these people was Betty Bone from the small New Forest village of Fordingbridge. Betty was used to jumping onto her bicycle and thought nothing of cycling to Southampton, some 30 odd miles away, to visit her family.

The road upon which she travelled, now called the B3078, was the occasional camp for groups of gypsies who would demand money from travellers using the road, if you didn't pay up then violence duly followed.

Upon hearing about the possible threat Betty's father decided to send her brother, and a friend, on the return journey to ensure that Betty returned home safely. As the trio cycled along merrily they became aware of a gentleman in front of them. He had appeared out of nowhere and seemed to be wearing outdated clothing; the thing of note that struck the trio was the gentleman's exceptional height which they estimated was roughly seven feet tall.

Hurtling past the unusual figure they thought no more about it. A quarter of a mile along the road the same mysterious man suddenly appeared again and only twenty paces in front of them.

Although now somewhat perplexed by their sighting of the same figure, who could not have possibly overtaken them, they cycled on. A further quarter of a mile along the road the trio encountered the same man yet again.

Now rather cautious of their encounter they cycled harder and faster in the attempt to escape the gentleman; they succeeded and he was witnessed no more on their eventual return back to Fordingbridge. Betty's brother and his friend did not encounter the figure on their way home that night either.

Who was the strikingly tall, out of fashion figure they saw? What was he doing there and possibly more importantly how was he ever able to overtake the friends without them noticing?

As this has been the only sighting of this ghost, to date, the answers to these questions may never be answered but should you be travelling along the B3078 in the future, keep an eye open for this man and see if you can get some answers from him!

CAMBRIDGE MILITARY HOSPITAL, ALDERSHOT

The town of Aldershot has always had a very strong military connection with the numerous barracks, housing the army, that have been constructed here since 1854; indeed Aldershot is known as "the home of the British Army".

With a strong military presence in the town it was logical to also build a military hospital. In fact Aldershot has five such hospitals and the Cambridge Military Hospital was the fifth to be built and welcomed its first patients on the 18th July 1879.

The ghost at this old hospital is, perhaps as one would expect, that of a nurse. The apparition has been spotted frequently, although usually at a distance, drifting along the exceptionally large corridors of the hospital.

Why has this nurse not left her post and why is she still here?

During the First World War the nurse's fiancée was admitted as a patient. Apparently the nurse became so upset at seeing her beloved injured and in pain that she had mistakenly given an overdose to her husband to be and it had killed him. Grief-stricken, the nurse took her own life.

You will notice that this legend has some very comparable similarities to the alleged ghost that haunted the Old Royal Victoria Military Hospital at Netley also in this book.

The most reliable and interesting of sightings of the ghostly nurse comes from 1969 when a Sister Collinson had noticed something by the bedside of a patient who was on the ward for the terminally ill. Sister Collinson was on her rounds and checked in on the patients who were, unfortunately, never going to leave the hospital alive when she noticed one of the patients, an elderly lady, was awake.

As she approached she noticed an empty glass of milk resting on the bedside cabinet of the patient and, knowing that milk was not readily available, she asked the lady where she had acquired it from.

The lady replied that she had awoken from her sleep and felt rather thirsty when she noticed a ward sister approaching her in a long grey and blue dress topped off with a scarlet red cape, the classic nursing uniform of the Queen Alexandra Royal Army Nursing Corp. This mysterious nurse placed the milk next to the patient and then left without saying a word.

The patient died shortly afterwards and who the kindly nurse was and why she was dressed in such an old style uniform was never discovered.

CHAWTON HOUSE, ALTON

One mile to the south west of the small town of Alton lays the picturesque village of Chawton.

When you visit the village and see its peace and tranquility you can instantly see why the famous Hampshire author Jane Austen chose to make her home here. Chawton House, now more commonly known as the Jane Austen House Museum, has been lovingly restored to exactly replicate the look and feel of the house as it was when Jane herself resided here; indeed the artifacts inside the museum are genuine items used by Jane in life and are not replicas.

With a house restored to its former historical appearance it's not uncommon to hear people reporting the feeling that Jane herself is about to enter a room, this could be down to pure psychological thought processes, but the sounds of footsteps and doors opening and closing on their own are not so easily explained.

Staff and visitors have in the past reported the feeling of being passed by an unseen presence; this has been reported both in the house and also the grounds surrounding Chawton House. One morning a member of staff was working in the house and became distracted by a noise that seemed to emanate from the garden. The staff member inspected the area but could find no explanation for the sound she had heard and so returned to her work. Upon entering the house she claims to have heard a distinct female voice whisper the word "Cass". Jane was very close to her sister, Cassandra, and the staff member concluded the voice could have been none other than the famous author herself, whispering the name of her beloved sister.

CHERITON BATTLEFIELD, ALRESFORD

On the 29th March 1644 the armies of the Parliamentarian officer Sir William Waller met with Sir Richard Hopton's Royalist forces in a field one mile to the east of the village of Cheriton, near Alresford. The ensuing battle raged all day long. The odds were stacked against the royalist forces with the Parliamentarian troops numbering some 10,000 to Hopton's 5,000.

At the end of the battle 300 of Hopton's forces lay dead and the Parliamentarians were successful in yet another conflict with the Royalists. It is said that if you wander the field where the battle took place, more specifically on the anniversary of the battle, you might be lucky enough to meet one of the long dead soldiers or even the whole army. The phantom battle is refought on fourth year of the anniversary with the last anniversary taking place in 2008. Should you be wandering the former battlefield on the 29th March 2012 and experience anything supernatural I would be delighted to hear from you.

COLONIAL BAR, HORNDEAN, PORTSMOUTH

The Colonial Bar, approximately twelve miles away from the main city centre of Portsmouth, is today a modern setting known for its great music and fantastic food but the bar also has a mysterious, supernatural side.

Sitting in the small civil parish of Horndean with its vibrant and chic environment it seems a little out of place but is very popular with people looking for a great night out but the staff here have experienced more than just the normal run of the mill occurrences one would expect in a bar of this nature.

Strange lights, sudden drops in temperature and orbs being photographed in their plenty are only the start of what else has been experienced here. Staff members working at the venue claim to have witnessed no less than four separate ghostly residents. The spectre of an elderly gentleman, a young girl dressed in a Victorian style dress and the apparition of a lady have all been reported. People also claim to have seen an ominous black humanoid shadow moving around the Colonial Bar.

One event in particular has caused alarm recently when a staff member was grabbed from behind by an unseen force, an event that still baffles reasonable explanation. Who and what haunts the bar is still unknown. Are they former residents of the bar from a time when its use was far flung from its current occupation or could they be connected to the old three storey workhouse that used to lay adjacent to the bar?

ECLIPSE INN, WINCHESTER

Dame Alicia Lisle is possibly Hampshire's most famous ghost.

Dame Lisle was a supporter of the Monmouth rebellion, although strongly denied by Dame Lisle herself, and when she was discovered sheltering two rebels in her home, Moyles Court near Ringwood, she was arrested and stood trial with the notorious Hanging Judge Jeffreys presiding.

Judge Jeffreys found Dame Lisle guilty and she was to be executed by being burnt at the stake but, after public outcry, the sentence was reduced to beheading. Dame Lisle spent her last night on this earth in one of her former homes, now a quaint little public house known as The Eclipse Inn, where the scaffolding for her execution was being built. The following morning Dame Lisle stepped from her bedroom window onto the scaffolding and the executioner did his job.

The ghost of Dame Lisle is said to still haunt the upper floors of the Eclipse Inn as well as her former home, Moyles Court in Ringwood and her former Parish church in Ellingham.

ELING TIDE MILL, ELING, TOTTON

The Eling Tide Mill is one of those, now becoming rarer, places where the visitor feels, upon entry, that they have been whisked back to a bygone era.

There has been a tide mill on this site for over 900 years, possibly even longer than this if the tide mill at Eling recorded in the Doomsday book of 1086 is the same venue, but much of the building that still stands to this day was constructed towards the end of the eighteenth and nineteenth centuries, the previous mill having sustained serious damage due to flooding.

When I visited the mill in May 2008 I spoke to Eling Tide Mill employee John Hurst whom retold me the story of their ghostly miller. "The ghost of a dead miller has been seen by people passing the building outside; they have reported seeing him looking through a window. Unfortunately I have been working here for over 6 years now and I have never seen him."

One would expect in a place such as this that the ghost occupying the building would be that of a former employee, from ages past and this is confirmed when further reports have been lodged by people who have witnessed the ghostly miller working in the sack loft. Unfortunately no one knows who the miller is or even when he worked at the mill; it seems that the spectre of the phantom miller is destined to grind wheat into flour for all eternity!

The Haunted Sack Loft at Eling Tide Mill.

Eling Tide Mill employee John Hurst standing at the window where the ghostly apparition of former miller has been witnessed by passers by.

EXPLOSION! MUSEUM, GOSPORT

The museum of naval firepower, known as Explosion! is an award winning £3.5 million discovery centre charting the development of naval weapons and is based in what used to be the store rooms where gunpowder was kept for Admiral Lord Nelson's impending battle with the French at Trafalgar.

Since the museum first opened its doors to members of the public, there have been many reports of paranormal phenomena taking place within its walls. Reports of flashing lights, disembodied moans, sensations of being touched and unexplained electro magnetic fluctuations abound.

Being a place where such a highly explosive substance such as gunpowder has been stored it's not surprising to hear of accidents at the site which have claimed the lives of those working here. There is even a story concerning a death that was caused by an alleged supernatural wind that was thought to have been the evil spirit of a former convict that died whilst working at the former stores.

Numerous paranormal investigation groups have conducted their own research at the museum and reports from people who claim to have seen the ghosts that haunt the former gunpowder depot are varied and include Royal Navy personnel based at the site, ghost hunters and security guards.

Explosion! is a venue that will hopefully give up more information and evidence of its supernatural secrets as time progresses.

FORT BLOCKHOUSE POINT, GOSPORT

John Aitkin. It's not a name that conjures up fame or fortune but this man's actions cost him his life and in some respects eternal fame. In 1776 John Aitkin, otherwise known as Jack the Painter, set fire to the Portsmouth rope house which supplied the Royal Naval fleet. John was arrested, found guilty and sentenced, at Winchester, to death by hanging.

John Aitkin was hung from the main mast of the *Arethusa*, a 38 gun frigate built in Bristol, in 1777 and his body was placed in a gibbet as a warning to all criminals. It is said that the rattling of Jack the Painter's chains can be heard ringing out from Blockhouse Point on stormy nights. For those with a more macabre interest in this story; visitors to Winchester's gate house museum can see the actual gibbet which was used to hang the carcass of Jack the Painter.

FORT BROCKHURST, GOSPORT

Not much is known of the apparition that haunts this nineteenth century fortification as he is never seen but he is heard on frequent occasions. Witnesses claim to hear the ghost wandering the numerous corridors of the fort, whistling as he goes about his business.

FORT GILKICKER, GOSPORT

Fort Gilkicker, located on the shoreline of Stokes Bay in Gosport, is yet another of Lord Palmerston's fabled defensive forts established to ward off a potential French invasion many decades ago.

The fort, now a former shadow of its once grand self, is derelict and in desperate need of conservation and restoration efforts but it is still home to a few select phantoms. The phantoms that exist in this property are that of a man and a woman and also a little girl who haunts the former accommodation block.

It is the ghost of the man who is the most intriguing though, for not only has he been seen from a distance but one security guard, working the late shift at the fort, actually confronted the ghost thinking it was an intruder. The security guard who I spoke to about his experience, to be known only as 'George' as he did not want his identity to be revealed, told me that one night he noticed a man standing underneath one of the security lights inside the walls of the fort. George approached the gentleman, thinking he was an intruder, to confront him about his presence in the fort, "what do you think you're doing in here, mate?" asked George. The man turned, faced George, and simply said, "not a lot" before vanishing into thin air.

Who these apparitions are and why they haunt the fort is unknown. Even if the names of the ghosts could be discovered, which is always difficult in most cases, the military records for this period of history are somewhat sparse in revealing as to where and when certain personnel were based and why.

Back in 2008 security guard Jason Humphries told me about a rather spooky experience he had whilst guarding the fort late one night. Jason was sitting in the security station, quietly watching the CCTV monitors, when he got the distinct impression he was being watched. Jason turned to face the window, which was only some

The haunted remains of Fort Gilkicker, Gosport, where the ghosts are no longer doomed to walk their former home for all eternity. © Askett Hawk.

three feet away from him, and imagine his shock and horror when he clearly saw three spectral faces peering through the window in at him. Thinking someone had illegally gained entry to the Fort Jason took off in hot pursuit of the would be intruders. When he reached the spot where the faces were seen at, which only took seconds to reach, there was no one present and the fort was as it should be... completely deserted!!

At the time of going to press I have received information from the owners of Fort Gilkicker who told me the Fort is due to undergo a period of renovation and conversion. All the ghosts that haunted Fort Gilkicker are now gone as they were successfully moved onto where they should be in early 2009.

FORT NELSON, PORTSMOUTH

Now home to the Royal Armouries Museum of Heavy Artillery, the Fort is haunted by just one solitary ghost.

A soldier who was once found to be drunk on duty was promptly arrested and placed in a cell pending a trial and court martial for his dereliction of duty.

Unable to cope with the remorse of his actions the soldier decided to take his own life. It is the soldier's spirit that has been blamed for feelings of unease and dread surrounding the area of the cells.....cells that every member of the public can visit to this day, so if you're visiting the Fort why not spend a little time here and see if you can feel what others have reported?

FORT PURBROOK, PORTSMOUTH, HAMPSHIRE

Standing on Portsdown Hill overlooking the city of Portsmouth is Fort Purbrook. This Fort was one of a series of forts that were commissioned, by the former Prime Minister, Lord Palmerston, as a defense against an impending French invasion, an invasion that never happened. The forts are now commonly referred to as Palmerston's follies.

Staff members working here have reported a series of spectral encounters including witnessing the ghost of a red coat sergeant but the most famous haunting is that of a small female child who goes by the name of Rosie. When the Fort was operational as a military establishment, officers and their families lived at the Fort and the ghost that is most commonly discussed is the child of one of these officers. It is said that the little girl wandered onto the ramparts to pet one of the Fort's sheep. As she leaned out to reach the animal she slipped and fell to the ground killing her instantly. Her story is often told to visitors at the Fort but sightings of the ghostly girl are not so common now.

FORT WIDLEY, PORTSMOUTH

Another of the Palmerston follies nestling quietly on Portsdown hill. In fact there is a large series of these forts covering Portsmouth and Gosport, but take a look into its ghosts and you will see it's still very much alive with spooks and spectres.

A ghostly drummer boy, spirits of French Napoleonic prisoners of war and poltergeist activity has all been reported at the Fort. Staff member Dave Hancock told me on one occasion how a member of their horse riding staff was doing their end of day duties in the stable block when she witnessed a leather strap literally throw itself across the corridor she was walking along. The spirit of an elderly lady has also been detected by mediums and psychics visiting the Fort, she mainly resides in two rooms that are now used for the Fort's murder-mystery events.

Gypsies Clump, Rowlands Castle

The area known today as Rowlands Castle has been inhabited for many centuries. There is evidence of Roman, Saxon and many other settlements, including a fourteenth century motte and bailey style of castle, from different eras of time and evidence from the past civilisations who made the village their home.

In an area known as Gypsies Clump, so called because of the area's former large gypsy settlement in the copse, haunts the ghost of a one Charlie Pearce.

Charlie was somewhat of a drunk and was often seen swigging from a kettle of gin, a habit that was to claim his life via a rather unfortunate accident. One day Charlie was riding through the copse and took a shot of his favourite tipple from his kettle. Not looking at where his horse was heading; Charlie failed to notice a large overhanging tree branch.

The branch struck Charlie across his throat and he fell from his horse. The damage was so severe to his throat that Charlie died upon the ground where he fell. People claim to have seen the ghost of Charlie wandering the woods where his unfortunate end occurred and he has also been seen both walking and riding towards the church.

Should you be lucky, or maybe even unlucky, enough to encounter the spirit of unfortunate, hapless Charlie he will be instantly recognisable to you, just look for the large weals across his ghostly throat, weals caused by the branch that claimed his life.

HAYMARKET THEATRE, BASINGSTOKE

The Haymarket Theatre in Basingstoke started its life as a corn exchange in 1837 but it has had many uses over the years from an ambulance station, ice skating rink, disco, bowling alley and was finally converted into a very popular theatre.

There are a variety of ghosts that allegedly haunt the boards of this theatre. The ghosts of three former employees, the spirit of a little girl, a man wearing a tricorn hat and cape, a grey lady and a mysterious whistling ghost that is often heard but never seen still lurk behind the theatre's walls.

When I investigated the theatre's haunting, back in 2003, a member of staff, Mrs. Jill Ward, was telling me of her own encounter with the paranormal. She was working in the administration block of the theatre and noticed a man walking towards her dressed in a tricorn hat and a long cape. Initially she thought it was a member of the acting staff dressed in his costume, this viewed changed though when the man passed the staff member and then walked straight through a closed door. Unfortunately for me, when I was investigating the theatre, I was not privy to another sighting of this particular individual but I did have a rather unusual encounter of my own.

I was on the stage directing the investigation proceedings when I looked up towards the auditorium seats. What I saw sitting there in the upper stalls, row D seat 6, was a male figure dressed in black with what appeared to be a large gaping wound across his throat. The theatre has no history of a sighting of this nature prior to mine and as far as I know I have been the only person to witness this strange looking ghost, exhibiting what appeared to be a painful looking wound. Was this a one off sighting, or simply my imagination, or is there perhaps more to be discovered at the theatre than we are currently aware off.

HMS VICTORY, PORTSMOUTH, HAMPSHIRE

HMS *Victory* was Admiral Nelson's flagship at the battle of Trafalgar and is to this day still a commissioned battleship in Royal Navy, although not seaworthy in the slightest sense.

Today the ship is in dry dock and is a popular tourist attraction in the city of Portsmouth where thousands of tourists come to see this fine battleship and the place where Lord Nelson died. As the ship is still owned by the Royal Navy its security staff are naval personnel. A retired sailor, who wished to remain anonymous, who worked as security on the ship has told me of some very strange happenings on board this historical vessel in the dead of the night.

In the ship's hull are replica barrels, replicas of the type used to store provisions for when the ship was at sea. These barrels are extremely large and very heavy taking between two to three people to move a single barrel. The former sailor told me on frequent occasions they would find the occasional barrel moved and placed at the top of a large flight of steps. Quite how these large and heavy barrels made their own way to the top of the stairs defies logical explanation. Members of staff have also reported seeing mysterious fleeting figures making their way around the decks of HMS *Victory* and unearthly sounds emanating from the ship where no living person is present.

HOPFIELD HOUSE, WATERLOOVILLE

In Donald A Parr's book, *Web of Fear*, the chapter on Hopfield House is titled "Buy Hopfield and Die" which seems a rather apt title giving Hopfield's notorious reputation as a house of misfortune.

The house is now somewhat hard to find amongst the urban sprawl that is now Waterlooville, just to the north of the city of Portsmouth. The setting was once very different as when the house was constructed here in the mid 1800s there was nothing in the immediate vicinity other than Hopfield, hence how the house got its name.

Built by Edward Fawkes, whose aim it was that the sprawling gothic looking mansion should always be occupied by his descendants alone, started life as a quiet countryside retreat. This changed however when Mr. Fawkes's son decided to put the house out to let after he left to occupy another house closer to his work in Southsea. The house was let to a retired naval officer and his wife who entertained their friends at the house and often dabbled with the occult there.

One evening the officer and his wife were stunned by a sudden sharp blast of cold wind and then the appearance of a ghost who identified himself as that of Edward Fawkes. The ghost threatened that occupants of Hopfield who were not his descendants would have no peace during their tenure. After sending written complaints about this spectral harassment to the owner the officer and his wife were permitted to leave and another tenant was found. The tenant this time was again a retired officer, a former captain in the British Army, and his wife. They lived happily in the house for some eight months before their tranquility was shattered when the captain was found dead with a dagger in his back and his wife was driven insane.

Some years later the house was bought by the affluent Nowell Family and it is this family that the true horror of Hopfields was unleashed upon. The Nowells had a son, who was by all accounts an intelligent outgoing man, who exhibited no signs of cares or worries. One day this happy go lucky son descended the staircase to the basement, loaded a shotgun and then proceeded to shoot himself in the head. The boy's mother was obviously overcome and distraught and shortly afterwards she died of a heart attack. His father then fell into deep depression, spurning the care offered to him by his daughter and friends. Soon after he was found dead in his bed. Was it natural causes that claimed Mr. Nowell's life or had the spectral form of Edward Fawkes played a part in his demise?

Many years later the house was converted into flats and from time to time I still get the occasional email from residents claiming that something untoward may still be lurking within the confines of Hopfield House.

HUHTAMAKKI FACTORY (FORMERLY POLARCUP), GOSPORT

A modern day production factory is not somewhere you would really expect to find ghosts but in this factory you can. The warehouse on the site is haunted by three male figures wearing World War II uniforms. Research into the history of the site shows that during World War II an anti aircraft gun emplacement and its crew were stationed on the ground that the warehouse now occupies. The emplacement took a direct hit from a German bomb, the gun and its crew were all destroyed. Perhaps the ghosts of the soldiers still think they are manning their long gone station; still defending the shores of England.

Workers at the factory to this very day claim to see the figures of the departed soldiers and are also treated, very occasionally, to the smell of freshly cooked phantom bacon.

HULBERT ROAD, WATERLOOVILLE

If you happen to be driving down Hulbert Road in Waterlooville and you come across a young lady walking on her own, it's probably prudent not to stop and offer her a lift as it could very well be the ghost of a phantom hitch hiker.

This apparition has been seen on numerous occasions and in the course of researching this book I had the fortune to come across two gentlemen, who wish to remain anonymous for fear of ridicule, who encountered this spirit one night. The two men were driving their car, after finishing work, down Hulbert Road on a rather wet and cold night when they noticed the lonely figure of a young woman walking at the side of the road.

One of the men suggested pulling over and picking her up but as they slowed down they could see that despite the heavy rain the girl was completely dry. Realising what they were seeing, the men accelerated away, and upon checking their rear view mirror the girl was no where to be seen.

HYDE TAVERN, WINCHESTER

Hyde Tavern, in Hyde Street, Winchester, is alleged to be the city's oldest public house and has therefore been welcoming guests seeking rest and refreshment for many centuries, however one of its patrons did not receive a cordial welcome and it is possible that this person's spirit haunts this quaint, small pub.

Tradition tells us that many years ago, unfortunately more precise records have been lost and this seems to be the case in many a tale of hauntings, that a poor woman once called at the Tavern begging for food and shelter. She was promptly refused both and continued on her way, and her body was found the following day after she had succumbed to hunger and the elements.

It is claimed that the ghost of this lady could be responsible for the haunting of the Hyde Tavern. Many guests over the years claim to have had their blankets pulled from their beds in the dead of night by some unseen, spectral force. Neatly stacked blankets have also been found scattered across the floor.

Perhaps the soul of this poor woman is seeking a little warmth from the blankets, warmth that was denied to her so many years ago.

ISLE OF WIGHT WAX MUSEUM, BRADING

As soon as you enter the Isle of Wight Wax Museum, now known as Brading the Experience, you cannot help but notice the intense historic and somewhat paranormal feel to the building.

Originally built as two houses they were knocked through to form one building for the creation of the museum in the 1960's. The museum is, without doubt, one of the most popular tourist attractions on the entire island. However, there is a darker side to this popular museum that many of its tourism cliental do not notice.

During the English Civil War, 1642-1651, a French emissary was sent to assist King Charles I in his escape from England. This emissary, Louis De Rochefort, took lodgings at the museum when it was a pub known as the Crown Inn.

It was to be Louis's last night on earth. His body was found the following morning. The exact cause of death has always been hotly debated, some suggest strangulation but others disagree with this. It's rumored that, whilst still clinging onto the last tattered shreds of life, Louis stated he would haunt the building until his mortal remains were returned to his beloved France.

Perhaps it is the spirit of Louis De Rochefort that has been witnessed over the years, haunting the museum and the area of the cottage garden. A tall, thin man wearing strange clothes has been reported over many years and it seems that Louis will continue to haunt the museum for many years to come as all attempts at tracing one of Louis's ancestors, in a bid to return his body to France, has, so far, all failed.

KEPPEL'S HEAD HOTEL, PORTSMOUTH
(See Sally Port Hotel, Portsmouth)

KING JOHN'S HOUSE, ROMSEY

Nestling down a lane, off Church Street in Romsey, lies King John's House. This medieval structure was first thought to be a hunting lodge used by King John when the Romsey area was nothing more than dense woodland, however, this theory has now been discontinued and it is believed the house was nothing more than a rather lavish merchant's house.

My connections to the house go back to 2002 and the site was initially chosen as the staff told me it was not haunted, the house was to be used as a testing ground for alleged mediums. After receiving the same specific psychic impressions from three different mediums on the same night, (none of the mediums had talked to each other) it was decided that in the light of the same information coming forward that we should commence a series of investigations at the site.

Over the next few years we encountered many strange and unexplainable phenomena, including the untying of securely fastened shoe laces, but there was one spirit who was very pronounced in the house. He only ever presented himself has a black shrouded figure and although seen by my investigators on numerous occasions he was very reluctant to communicate and somewhat annoyed at our presence.

We encountered three other spirits at the property, a man, a woman and a boy of around six to eight years of age. Our investigations at the site ended in 2008 when we decided that we had obtained all possible information and evidence from the house that we were going to get.

KINGS THEATRE, SOUTHSEA, PORTSMOUTH

The Kings Theatre first drew back its performance curtain in 1907 and has been one of the most popular theatres in the area ever since. Perhaps it's because of the theatre's excellent series of plays, dramas and comedies that the mysterious apparition of a man in brown has been seen and refuses to move onto pastures new.

Technical staff at the theatre some years ago left an audio recorder running overnight in the hope of capturing any unusual sounds that any possible ghosts may make. They recorded lots of "natural sounds" such as wood creaking, but there was one incident that was not so easy to explain away and that was the single note of a piano key being struck.

LEIGH ROAD, EASTLEIGH

On the corner of Leigh Road in Eastleigh is a phone box, nothing unusual in that I hear you say, but the phone box has a somewhat strange reputation.

People passing by have heard the phone ringing; they pick it up to answer the call, because as we all know a ringing phone demands to be answered. Those that answer the call claim that a message is given to them that is so terrifying they dare not repeat what has been said during the conversation.

I have many issues relating to this story. If the call is so distressing why do people stop to answer the phone even though the terrifying tale is well known? What words can be spoken to elicit such fear? And could these terrifying calls be attributed to local children playing a prank?

Until someone speaks up and revels what the mysterious caller is telling its victims I don't think the riddle of the haunted phone box will ever be solved. I would be very happy to classify this legend as that.....nothing more than a local, urban legend.

MARWELL HALL, COLDEN COMMON

Marwell Hall, now part of the Marwell Zoological Gardens, has an immense history. It is said that King Henry VIII proposed to Jane Seymour here once he had received the news on the beheading of Queen Anne Boleyn.

With such a history it is not surprising that it also has numerous legends and ghost stories. The hall and grounds are said to be haunted by spirits of Roundheads and Cavaliers who perished here during a skirmish. It is also said that the reenactment of the battle can be seen in the area on its anniversary of 3rd March.

Near to the hall is the Kudu enclosure and staff at the zoo have told me that the Kudu exhibit some strange behavior at times. "They seem to stand, stare and follow something moving down the path that we just can't see" stated one staff member who wished to remain anonymous. In recent years the sounds of civil war drums have actually been recorded on digital audio devices and experts in the history of the civil war period analyzed these drumming sounds and said "it's definitely civil war drums, it's a call to arms drum roll."

Among Marwell Hall's repertoire of ghosts there are the ghosts of children, former residents, a group of monks and of course no stately home would be complete without its mistletoe bride. In the mistletoe bride legend it is stated that a bride on her wedding day was playing hide and seek and she chose to hide in a large oak chest in a seldom used part of the hall. The chest was a self locking type, trapped inside, the bride subsequently died of suffocation.

Her remains were found by workmen years later, the discovery of a skeleton in a wedding gown must have caused a very intense element of shock. This mistletoe bride legend is attached to many old homes throughout the United Kingdom and it seems the story has its origins in Italy although cases of the mistletoe bride have even been reported as far off as the United States of America.

MASTER BUILDERS HOUSE HOTEL, BUCKLER'S HARD

This delightful hotel, located on Beaulieu River and adjacent to the historical ship building village of Buckler's Hard, has a somewhat sorrowful spectre.

I had the pleasure of discussing the hotel's ghost with a former front of house manager. He told me that on frequent occasions guests had asked to be moved from their room to an alternative room because of the appearance of a sad looking woman who was also accompanied by an intense sorrowful atmosphere.

Legend tells us that a woman who once lived in the hotel threw her newborn baby from an upper window, killing the child instantly and dooming her to an eternity at the hotel.

The appearance of the ghost was even mentioned in Alec Holland's book Buckler's Hard: A Rural Shipbuilding Centre. The entry reads:

During the nineteenth century, several inhabitants of the Master Builder's House 'saw' a ghost on the stairs and in one of the bedrooms. Ellen Smith, daughter of Lord Montagu's river bailiff, who lived in the house in 1901, described a visitation as follows, 'a lady fair and rather nice looking, with such a sad face and light eyes which seemed to say help me…it is a sad face in a grey dress, light hair, about 28 or 30'. Who else but Elizabeth Adams, née Smith?

The lady referred to as Elizabeth Adams in the story may well be the identity of the ghost but without further paranormal research into this matter it is, at this time, only speculation.

Historical sources reveal no death of a child at the hotel, natural or otherwise, and it appears that this may be yet another unsolved mystery begging for closure.

MEDIEVAL MERCHANT'S HOUSE, SOUTHAMPTON

If you walk down French Street, in the City of Southampton, one of the first things that you notice is the lack of buildings that front onto the road. The reason for this is that most of this street was levelled, courtesy of the Luftwaffe during World War II, but one particular house of interest remains.

Built in 1290, for wine merchant John Fortin, as a shop and home, the Medieval Merchant's House oozes history and a distinctly spooky atmosphere.

The Medieval Merchant's House has had many uses over the years, as all historical buildings appear to have had, from being a lodging house to a public house known as The Bull and then finally became a brothel.

It is from the building's time as a brothel that the ghost story, or at least a majority of it, stems from. It is claimed that a prostitute who worked here was quite fond of murdering her clients for their valuables, namely jewellery. One time, after she had dispatched her sailor employee, she removed his valuables and for some unknown reason proceeded to throw them down a well.

During the 1950s the Medieval Merchant's House was hired by an amateur dramatics group, known as the student players, and was used as their rehearsal rooms, store and workshop. One night the budding actors and actresses decided to hold a séance and they allegedly contacted the spirit of the murdering prostitute who told them she was named Ruth Dill.

During this séance, Ruth Dill, revealed the details of her murdering antics and told the participants that she hid valuables down the well. One of the men involved in the séance claimed it was all rubbish and at that time a table that was being used for the séance smashed into a wall. Thinking that this apparent, violent display of paranormal ability indicated the site of the well, the members of the Student Players started a search for the well ... they didn't find the well and to date no well is known at the house.

Who haunts the house is still a mystery and suspect to speculation but it does not detract from the fact that previous owners have witnessed a female figure, standing at the foot of their beds, as well as candles being blown out and doors opening and closing on their own.

Does the restless spirit of a murderous prostitute still haunt Southampton's Medieval Merchant's House?

MOTTISFONT ABBEY, NEAR STOCKBRIDGE

This beautiful former abbey, now open to the public and renowned for its rose gardens, possesses an apparition that can appear as virtually anything.

The east lawn is a part of the garden where it has been reported, by previous owners of the house, that if an apparition is encountered then death will befall the person who witnesses it within one year. The ghost has appeared as both male and female apparitions and the last firmly recorded sighting was on the 27th December 1897.

Two brothers were walking across the garden, tracking the flight paths of geese, when one of the gentlemen, referred to only as Dan, commented on someone walking across the lawns. It was only Dan that had seen the figure. Six weeks later....Dan was dead.

The spectre of Mottisfont only appears to the first born son and legend leads us to believe it's a harbinger of death. I visited the Abbey in February 2007 and when I left at around 2 am both myself and two staff members witnessed a figure walking up the drive to the gate. At first the staff thought it was the groundkeeper but when they enquired the following day the gentleman claimed, "it wasn't me." So who was the mysterious figure we witnessed? So far none of us who witnessed this figure has died...yet!

MOYLES COURT, RINGWOOD

Moyles Court is the former home of Dame Alicia Lisle but today is used as a boarding school. During the Monmouth rebellion of 1685 Dame Lisle was arrested, on the charge of harboring traitors, after it was discovered that she provided shelter to two well known non-conformists, John Hickes and Richard Nelthorpe. The presiding judge at her trial, the now infamous Hanging Judge Jeffreys, condemned her to death by being burnt at the stake; this was commuted to beheading after public outrage.

Dame Alicia Lisle was executed in the market place, Winchester, on the 2nd September 1685 and her ghost has been reported both at Moyles Court and the lanes leading to and from her former home. Some reports claim the ghost is headless with her head tucked in regal fashion neatly under her arm. (*See also* Eclipse Inn, Winchester and Ellingham Church, Ringwood.)

The smell of violets has often been detected over the years which many have attributed to the ghost of Dame Lisle. One of the strangest of events in recent years was the apparent re-arranging of furniture in a room that was securely locked.

MUSEUM OF ARMY FLYING, MIDDLE WALLOP

The Museum of Army Flying is about more than just aircraft. A replica 1940's house, simulators, rifle ranges and a cinema are all hands on experiences that visitors can try in this innovative and varied museum.

Without a doubt it is the museum's 35 historic aircraft that are the main attractions, but keep an eye out for its ghosts.

The ghost of a former Women's Auxiliary Air Force employee has been seen riding her bicycle, the ghost of a small boy playing in one of the museums helicopters and the sounds of footsteps on the mezzanine floor have all been reported.

Recently the museum has opened its doors to paranormal investigators looking at solving the mysteries of the museum's ghosts and with time, I dare say, more information will come to light regarding its ghosts.

NETLEY ABBEY, NR SOUTHAMPTON, HAMPSHIRE

Netley Abbey, a religious monastery founded in 1239 by Peter des Roches, the Bishop of Winchester from 1205–1238, is a former Cistercian abbey settled by monks from nearby Beaulieu Abbey.

One of the most famous legends concerning a haunting at the abbey centres around a ghost by the name of Blind Peter. It is said that during the dissolution of monasteries, under Henry VIII in 1538, the abbey's wealth was hidden down a secret tunnel and one lone monk was left behind to guard the treasure. Many people over the years have set about the discovery of this tunnel and its immense wealth but none have ever found it, except that is for a gentleman named Slown.

Slown went in search of the mythical tunnel and when he found an entrance to an underground passage it was thought the treasure might at last have been found. Upon entering the passageway Slown vanished into the darkness only to emerge minutes later screaming "In the name of God, block it up!" He then collapsed and died. The passageway was subsequently resealed and all note of its location has been lost.

In 1719 the abbey passed into the ownership of Walter Taylor who started the demolition of various parts of the abbey to use as building materials for other structures in the local area. As soon as the work commenced Taylor was plagued by dreams of a ghostly monk warning him of his impending doom if the demolition, and therefore the desecration of the once mighty abbey, was not halted. Taylor chose to ignore these warnings and during a routine inspection of the work taking place a part of the east window arch fell on top of Taylor causing a serious amount of injury to his head. Mr. Taylor subsequently died from his injury and work was halted, no one else wanted to risk that wrath of the phantom monk.

I too have had my own encounter with the undead whilst investigating Netley Abbey back in 2002. The report of my experience is logged in my archives as follows:

We had finished for the night, myself and the three investigators present, and all equipment was packed away. We went for a final walk around to ensure no rubbish was left behind and the site was exactly how we found it.

We passed the Chapter House and a member of my team said "someone's just gone in there"

We looked inside with the torches switched on but saw nothing.

When we switched the torches off something appeared on the floor....it looked like a large Hessian cloth with something wriggling underneath it... when we switched on the torches it vanished....when they were switched off.....it was there.

I remember watching it intently and then something emerged out of the cloth. To be honest it was horrific.

Large bulbous head, large skewer like teeth, oval eyes and extremely thin. It moved and faced us....it reached out its arm and we moved backwards.... the things arm just stretched and stretched.

There's some major points that I remember about that night which help us understand that hallucination or poor lighting could not have made us misinterpret something completely natural.

• Clear Night with ¾ moon – plenty of light
• Seen by four investigators – all explained the same sighting
• Seen by four investigators – from four different angles
• Why was it seen with no torch light?

No one has been able to explain what we saw that night although I have subsequently heard that others after us have reported seeing the same apparition in the chapter house......no one knew our results so they couldn't have been persuaded by prior suggestion."

NEW KING STREET, PORTSMOUTH

This haunting is directly linked to a private residence in the street and at their request the exact address has to remain anonymous.

The area that New King Street now occupies used to be where the Corona lemonade factory was established on the site back in the 1800s. One resident in particular has reported the sighting in her flat of a young boy dressed in Victorian style clothing, although somewhat dirty looking; the owner has also reported the sounds of a horse drawn carriage pulling into where the owner's garage now stands.

Research and investigation into this property and haunting revealed that the boy is believed to be a Victorian stable hand. This conclusion coincided with further information which discovered that the owner's garage is actually situated on what was the stabling for the horses and storage area for the carts that used to distribute the lemonade made at the factory.

It seems that the ghostly carts pulling heavy loads of lemonade still rumble through the ages in an attempt to make their delivery and the stable boy.....he's happy where he is and so is the owner and to this day I am aware that they live side by side in relative peace and harmony.

NEW PARK MANOR HOTEL, BROCKENHURST

If you should holiday in the New Forest then you must stay at the New Park Manor Hotel on Lyndhurst Road, Brockenhurst.

This stylish former country house, once frequented by King Charles and Nell Gwyn as it was their favourite hunting lodge, not only offers extremely luxurious accommodation, spa, outdoor pool, equestrian centre and croquet lawn but can also boast some magnificent ghostly occurrences.

The sound of mumbled voices have been reported. Paranormal investigators claim to have witnessed an unexplained figure in one of the hotels passageways and sudden supernatural footsteps and the sounds of a panting animal have all been reported over the years.

The oldest part of the hotel are the eleventh century cellars and many people claim to feel a presence in the area, although the ghost that haunts this area has never been witnessed, dogs refuse to enter and some claim an unwelcome feeling connected to the entity in the cellar.

The hotel's other ghosts are somewhat more welcoming though. The sound of an approaching coach and horses is heard rumbling past, and even felt underfoot. The apparition of an elderly gentleman dressed in a black suit has been seen frequenting the lounge and restaurant both in the daytime and at night. A lady originating from the 1700s has been seen looking from the windows of the public rooms, which were once her front room, and a lady attired in a green dress has been seen looking out from one of the bedroom windows which used to be a nursery. The strangest element about this ghostly lady is the fact that she is staring out of a window that no longer exists...in essence she is staring into a solid brick wall.

The final ghost at the hotel haunts one of the bedrooms and many people do not stay in this room as they often report a feeling of unease and dislike about the room, which is probably for the best. The only person to have seen the ghost, that of the crouching maid, in this room stated that she was accompanied by a disgusting smell and grotesque teeth...she probably had a hard life so if you are the next person to see this ghostly maid don't treat her too harshly.

NEW THEATRE ROYAL, PORTSMOUTH

The New Theatre Royal in Guildhall Walk is haunted by the ghost of an actor who somehow managed to slit his own throat here in the 1880s.

One of the backstage dressing rooms is haunted by this apparition and it is claimed that the actor who killed himself used the very same dressing room.

ODIHAM CASTLE, BASINGSTOKE

Odiham Castle is now nothing more than a shell of its once former glory.

Construction started in 1204 and the castle eventually became the seat of the Montfort family who became very powerful after the marriage of Simon de Montfort to King John's daughter, Eleanor, in 1238. The castle was also used as a prison to house the Scottish King, and son of the famed Robert the Bruce, David.

Despite its many high profile connections the castle is not haunted by anyone famous. No spectral kings or queens here but the lonely wraith of a wandering minstrel has been reported frequently.

Described as wearing shreds and patches the phantom minstrel is accompanied by the sound of music as he pipes away on some unknown instrument.

Local residents also claim to have witnessed the apparitions of former prisoners, which were held at the castle, moving around the ruins before inexplicably disappearing.

OLD WINCHESTER HILL, CORHAMPTON

Rather confusingly called Old Winchester Hill even though it is situated some eleven miles away from Winchester, in the East Meon Valley, just adds to the magic of this ancient site.

Formerly known as Old Windover Hill the site is a former Iron Age Hill Fort and Bronze Age Cemetery, the outline of the fort and the barrows contained within it are clearly visible from a short distance, it is today popular with dog walkers, ramblers and budding archaeologists whom you will find kicking over the upturned mole hills in the search for pottery shards.

Even though the hill has many visitors throughout the year there has been only one reported sighting of a paranormal encounter on the hill itself. Lying around the outskirts of the fort there are numerous small copses, thickets and bushes, two visitors returning from a day of walking around the site left the fort and cut through the valley lying beneath the hill. On cutting through this valley they passed a small patch of woodland and came only a few feet away from the apparitions of a man and a woman.

One of the witnesses told me "It took us totally by surprise, we turned the corner and right in front of us was a man and woman. The man was standing, holding what looked like a spear, and dressed in a type of tartan cloak, the woman was dressed in a similar fashion but was seated."

The couple stood there in amazement before the ghosts faded from view. Later on they decided to look up the history of the fort and the peoples that once inhabited the site. They quickly came across artists' impressions of Iron Age people dressed in exactly the style they had witnessed.

They continued; "We had no interest in ghosts or history but this experience, which totally has us confused, has certainly made us think about an afterlife and what happens after we die. After all, if it wasn't ghosts we saw that day, then what was it?"

PALACE HOUSE, BEAULIEU

Palace House is the former main gatehouse of the once grand Beaulieu Abbey. The house has been greatly modified throughout the years, since the abbey's dissolution in 1538, and remains the ancestral home of the Montagu family.

Being connected to the once great abbey itself it is hardly surprising that the ghostly wraiths of the former monks have been witnessed inside the home but there is also a plethora of other unexplainable occurrences inside the house. The smell of incense and the sounds of Gregorian chanting have been heard within the many walls of the stately mansion and the apparition of a lady in blue, commonly thought to be a former family member, Countess Isabella, has been reported.

A footman tending the fire in the portrait gallery, a ghostly woman sitting in a window seat in the lower drawing room, a ghostly cavalier and a phantom dog that likes to sit on the staircase have also been reported by people visiting the property.

If you tour the house, as the venue is open to members of the public; you will discover a small secret staircase. You can access the first part of this staircase but the rest of it is unfortunately closed to the public. At the top of this staircase there is a small room where it is alleged that a cavalier, probably the same cavalier whose ghost has been seen elsewhere in the house, was slain by his roundhead enemy and it is theorised that this room is now home to this somewhat foreboding ghost. People staying in the room report a feeling of dread and do not feel at ease, in fact a former family friend who stayed in this room one night fled the house in terror and refused to stay in the house again, or even talk of what she had encountered during her brief stay in the room.

To get to the secret staircase you have to ascend the family's magnificent main staircase which seems to be a focal point in seeing fleeting apparitions and shadows.

If you ascend the staircase be watchful for the third stair up. This is meant to be the resting place of a ghostly German Shepherd dog. Many people claim to have come down the stairs, tripped and fell over something they say felt like they had stood on a dog. The strange factor with this story is that those who know of the ghost dog's liking for this step never seem to take a fall over it, those with no knowledge of its presence are the ones falling victim to the slumbering canine.

The estate contacted me recently about a very bizarre occurrence. A member of the public was taking photos of the portraits in the lower portrait gallery when all of a sudden he screamed and ran out of the house. The staff working in the house pursued him and asked him what on earth the matter was. He stated that as he looked through the eyepiece of his camera, viewing one of the portraits he was about to photograph; he had seen a face leave the portrait and fly towards him. The event scared the man so much he refused to re-enter the house.

The ancestral home of the Montagu family and the home of an assortment of ghostly encounters.

There is a story connected to the house about a butler and a maid. It was alleged the maid was pregnant with the butler's child and when he discovered this he decided to take his revenge on the hapless maid. As she made her way down the stairs, going about her daily duties, the butler is said to have pushed her so hard down the steep staircase that the maid died instantly when she hit the floor. Although this event has not been documented in the historical record, in all fairness no intensive records of servants working in a house of this nature are common place, members of the public visiting the house and staff working here do report seeing a mysterious black figure on the stairs and in the staff room, they also report the occasional feeling of being shoved in the back when they descend the staircase, is the ghostly butler still up to his murderous antics or is legend running wild?

One former staff member claims to have witnessed a female spectre dressed as a maid ascending the staircase. Thinking it was a living member of staff, reenacting the role of a time gone by, she was rather shocked when the phantom maid vanished in front of her very eyes.

It should be noted that many books retelling the ghost stories of Hampshire often claim that it is the main staircase that the murder took place on but the staff at the estate have informed me that the murder took place on a very steep cement staircase which is not open to members of the public. This is only theorised though as no firm records exist of this murder....even if it did occur?

PALMERSTON RESTAURANT, ROMSEY, HAMPSHIRE

Strange banging sounds, lights switching themselves on and off for no apparent reason, toilets flushing, doors opening of their own volition, feelings of being watched and the occasional shove in the back are all phenomena attributed to Charlie, the ghost of an old man who haunts the upper floors of the Palmerston restaurant.

No one knows who Charlie is and why he haunts the restaurant and sightings of him have diminished throughout the years which mean that we will probably never get to the bottom of the mystery surrounding the haunting of the Palmerston Restaurant. The haunting may be attributed to an event that occurred a short distance away in what was the Swan Inn, now the Romsey conservative club.

In 1642 two roundhead soldiers were hung from a makeshift gallows, which was the sign bracket of the Swan Inn which can still be seen in place hanging outside the building. One of the soldiers allegedly managed to free himself and flee down an alleyway, but his bid for freedom was short-lived as he died in the alleyway. The Palmerston Restaurant now occupies the area where the soldier met his hellish death, perhaps this deathly event may well have some contributing factor to the haunting of the restaurant.

PORTCHESTER CASTLE, PORTSMOUTH

Portchester Castle has seen its fair share of history. Everyone from the Romans to medieval monarchs have used or visited the castle, indeed the castle has the highest most complete standing roman walls in Europe, outside Italy.

The castle has been used primarily as a military base but during the Napoleonic wars it housed hundreds of prisoners of war. Mediums and psychics claim their spirits still haunt the area of the keep, and later it was used as a rubbish tip. When I investigated the castle in 2002 was I was expecting to be greeted with a whole host of ghost stories but this is not the case. I met with Alan Blondel, one of the castle's custodians, and he told me about the apparition of a white clad figure that had been witnessed and has been well documented in other books concerning ghosts of Hampshire.

It turns out that this apparition was nothing more than a practical joke that a gentleman played on his friends in the early 1900s and the whole joke has steam rolled out of control. There are reports of a brown clad monk, which is entirely believable as a priory also exists in the castle confines. It has been seen emerging from a barred gate to the left of the land gate but this spectre did not put in an appearance for me.

One ghost did however. It was about 8 pm and I arrived at the castle with a friend who shot off to the local shop to buy something to eat. No sooner had he left I noticed an incredibly large figure dressed totally in black, with no discernable features, standing on the walkway to the right of the land gate. The figure promptly disappeared and did not put in another appearance throughout the rest of the night.

Mr. Blondel also told me of an experience he had one night when he was locking up the castle, after a busy day of welcoming excited tourists to the romantic ruins. "I was walking along the courtyard to lock up the keep when I heard this almighty crash, it was so loud I thought one of the keep's walls had fallen down."

The wall hadn't fallen down and to this day no explanation has been forthcoming for the origin of this sound.

The keep of Porchester Castle where it is claimed that the spirits of former Napoleonic prisoners of war still haunt to this very day.

RED LION INN, HORNDEAN

Much of the historical atmosphere of the Red Lion Inn at Horndean has now been lost due to a modern renovation of the building some years ago now. I suppose it's better that an historical building remains rather than it fall into disrepair and finally demolition.

The pub is haunted by both a young lady and an old lady. The old lady is believed to be a one Mrs. Byden who once lived at the pub. When Mrs. Byden passed from this life into the next world her body was removed from the Red Lion in a somewhat disrespectful manner. It was not possible to move her remains downstairs and through the front door, so she was winched out of the building from an upstairs window. Perhaps this method of removing her from her former home is what has given rise to the haunting in the first instance.

The spectral form of an elderly lady has been seen frequently over the years, especially so on the staircase, and residents and patrons have reported a wide series of paranormal occurrences including doors opening and closing, latches lifting and dropping of their accord and people sensing they have been touched by an unseen presence.

Who the young lady is no one appears to know, investigators and researchers over the years have speculated they are two separate entities or perhaps both ghosts are Mrs. Byden at different times of her life.

RED LION INN, SOUTHAMPTON

The Red Lion Inn, which is situated on the High Street in Southampton city centre, has its origins laying in the twelfth century, although much of the building that still stands to this day is Tudor in origin. One of the pubs former uses was that of a courtroom and many a criminal was put on trial at the building, found guilty and led 200 yards to the nearby Bargate, still a popular tourist attraction which houses visiting exhibitions of interest, where they were hung by the neck until their earthly lives came to an end.

Probably the most famous of the pub's visitors was none the less than King Henry V who stopped at the inn, when it was a court, to preside over the trial of three conspirators. Henry found the conspirators guilty and passed the death sentence upon them. Perhaps the sorrowful ghostly funeral procession that has been sighted making its way from the Red

Lion Inn towards the Bargate is for these wretched souls whose lives ended before their time.

There is also one other spectre associated with the venue though. The pub allegedly has the ghost of a former female employee. She has been sighted, mainly, on the small staircase, or at least that is where most of the staff over the years have witnessed her, that leads to an upper seating area, the same area where the judges passed sentence many years ago.

The Red Lion public house in Southampton where a ghostly funeral procession is said to leave from and head towards the Bargate, Southampton's former place of execution.

ROUNDABOUT COTTAGE, BRAMSHOTT

A few years after the famous horror actor, Boris Karloff, moved back to England he and his wife found a cottage in the Hampshire village of Bramshott which they moved into.

The cottage had never had a reputation of being haunted but all that changed when Boris Karloff departed this mortal world on the 2nd February 1969 after a short battle with pneumonia brought on from long term suffering of arthritis and emphysema.

Since his death the ghost of Boris has been reported to haunt the old cottage and people claim to have heard his ethereal voice disappearing as quickly as it had appeared.

ROUNDABOUT HOTEL, FAREHAM

You can not help but notice the Roundabout Hotel in Fareham, a large black and white building nestling on a slip road leading to the M27 motorway, and an overnight stay here may well be further enjoyed if you encounter its spectre.

The ghost of small boy, aged between 12 to 13 years of age, wearing a black jacket, buckled shoes, blonde hair and sporting a childish grin was frequently seen in the 1970s.

It is said his appearance was heralded by a sudden decrease in temperature.

Sightings of this ghostly youth have diminished in recent years following a fire which destroyed part of the building.

ROYAL MARINES MUSEUM, PORTSMOUTH

The Royal Marines Museum in Southsea, Portsmouth was for many years a major pivotal barracks in the history of the Royal Marines; it was here that the men underwent training who eventually became known as the cockleshell heroes.

Despite the thousands of troops and officers who passed through its gates, the museum is home to just two ghosts. One of these has been seen haunting the area around the main stairs which enter the museum. It is the ghost of a little girl who, it is claimed, ran in front of a horse and carriage approaching the barracks and was crushed to death underneath the weight of the horse and carriage.

Many of the staff at the museum do not like entering the attic and it is here where a most tragic event once occurred. During the 1800s an officer by the name of Wolf was stationed here, and he was engaged in a relationship with an unknown woman. It is claimed that she ended this relationship, and in a fit of despair Colonel Wolf ascended the stairs to the attic, burnt the love letters his beloved had sent him and then promptly shot himself in the head with his service revolver. Staff have claimed to encounter a depressing atmosphere in the very room where this tragedy occurred, even new members of staff who know nothing of the story have even reported this feeling, and the smell of burning paper has also been commented on and reported.

Perhaps Colonel Wolf's emotions have become imprinted into the fabric of the building, but what of the smell of burning paper. Is the colonel still there burning his love letters in a twisted turn of fate?

Royal Victoria Military Cemetery, Netley

Containing nearly 800 burials of the dead from the Crimean war, World War I and World War II it's hardly surprising that reports of paranormal activity have been alleged at the cemetery, especially so when you consider the often tragic and violent deaths experienced by those entombed within its seventeen acres of consecrated grounds.

Visitors to the cemetery, in the dead of the night, claim to have witnessed black shadowy figures, heavy footsteps as if a group of people are marching around the area with boots on and the sounds of machine gun fire have also been recorded on dictaphones by investigators examining the area and its activity.

Royal Victoria Military Hospital, Netley

Located approximately ¾ of a mile away from the Royal Victoria Military cemetery is the site of the former Royal Victoria Military Hospital. Nowadays nothing more than a field occupies the site and the only surviving part of the former hospital is the chapel, which is open to members of the public.

The hospital was laid down on the 19th May 1856 by Queen Victoria herself and when completed it was some 1,424 feet in length and had 1000 beds spread over its 138 wards. It is from the time when the doctors and nurses were in their abundance at the hospital that a ghostly nurse legend originates from.

Legend leads us to believe that a nurse at the hospital fell in love with a patient in her care and that she accidently administered an overdose which killed the patient in question. Absolutely devastated at her mistake the nurse took her own life. There is another twist in this tragic tale though and like many ghost stories there is an alternative, possible story. Revolving around the same nurse loved a patient story, it's claimed that the nurse discovered an affair between her beloved and another nurse, becoming jealous and angry at the discovery the nurse administered her lover an overdose, but on this occasion on purpose. The story ends the same way with the nurse committing suicide. Many patients claimed to have witnessed this spectral nurse over the years and strangely enough virtually all the stories revolve around one particular ending. When the nurse was seen standing at the foot of the bed of a patient then that person was soon to die. The nurse was no longer a caring, much needed medical assistant but more a harbinger of death to fear and at all costs to avoid.

During the demolition of the old hospital in 1966 workmen on site frequently downed tools and refused to continue work, as the recurrent sighting of a ghostly woman in an old nurse's uniform was too much for many of the men to bear.

RUFUS STONE, BROOK, NEW FOREST

The small New Forest town of Cadnam has its own royal ghost. The Rufus stone, which is located a mile and half from Cadnam, marks the spot where on the 2nd August 1100AD King William Rufus was accidentally shot by an arrow, fired by his friend, Sir Walter Tyrell during a hunting party.

The king's body was taken by horse and cart through a track way leading to Winchester and it is said that the sound of horses hooves and the rumble of the cart wheels can still be heard following this track way. Maybe he his still making his way to Winchester for his burial which occurred hundreds of years ago although he seems to be blissfully unaware of this fact.

One night in 2008, soon after the anniversary of the king's death, I was investigating an unrelated case in the area and myself and three investigators all heard the strange and unusual sound of horse hoofs being followed by the rumble of a wheel over a gravel path!

To this day I have not been able to find a rational and conclusive explanation.

The Rufus Stone monument marks the place of the tree that Sir Walter Tyrell fired his fatal arrow from.

SALLY PORT HOTEL, PORTSMOUTH

Sitting directly adjacent to the large and sprawling shopping complex of Gunwharf Quays sits the Sally Port Hotel.

The hotel claims its resident ghost is none other than Lionel "Buster" Crabb, a Lieutenant Commander in the Royal Navy who specialised as a frogman. In 1956 Buster Crabb was sent down to investigate the hull of the battle cruiser *Ordzhonikidze*, which had docked in Portsmouth harbour carrying Nikita Khrushchev & Nikolai Bulganin on a diplomatic mission.

Buster never returned from his mission and his body was found washed ashore on Pilsey Island, near Chichester, just over a year later. The corpse was headless and had both hands cut from its body. Identification of the body was difficult but was indentified as the body of Buster after a friend noticed a scar on the corpse's knee, a scar that Buster also bore.

It is said that Mr. Crabb's last night on our little blue planet was spent in the Sally Port Hotel, a claim also shared by another nearby hotel known as the Keppel's Head, and that his ghost has been felt wandering the building, in another twist to this story it appears that Buster's residency at either hotel cannot be confirmed as the pages of their registers, for both hotels, have mysteriously been torn out on the day he had allegedly stayed.

SELBORNE PRIORY, ALTON

These days Selborne, a small village parish near Alton, is more famous for its associations with Gilbert White, an eighteenth century naturalist and ornithologist, than its ghosts, but there are at least two ghosts in the village that are well worth mentioning.

Priory Farm now stands on the spot of a former Priory, Selborne Priory, which was closed in 1485 due to incurring some very large debts. It is said that the ghostly monks still wander the site of their long gone priory.

A phantom dog is also said to wander the priory looking for a friend of his, not an owner as one would expect but rather unusually the dog was an inseparable companion to a local racehorse that was trained nearby. The dog was unfortunately killed in an accident and local legend tells us that the dog is still looking for his, now long gone, friend.

SIR WALTER TYRELL PUBLIC HOUSE, BROOK, NEW FOREST

This popular New Forest public house takes its name from a most unfortunate person.

Sir Walter Tyrell was out hunting with his friend, King William Rufus, on the 2nd August 1100AD when an arrow fired from his bow, intended for a passing deer, accidently struck the king and killed him.

A former employee at the pub has told me there is a certain ominous male entity pervading its very walls. A disembodied voice shouting "Get out" has been heard by staff and a local medium from the area has told of her sighting of a gentleman whose favourite haunt seems to be the area surrounding the fireplace.

The Sir Walter Tyrell pub in Brook, staff working here claim to have heard a disembodied voice shouting "Get Out".

The house next to the pub also has a haunted reputation. In September 2008 I was contacted by two amateur ghost hunters who decided to check out the house one night. They become somewhat scared when a door closed on its own, probably due to wind passing through one of the houses many broken windows, so they decided to leave the house and return another time. Before leaving they decided to take some photos of the outside of the house and noticed the spectre of an elderly looking woman peering out from a downstairs window.

Even to this day they have not been able to explain their experience but perhaps the woman was just watching to ensure the two would be intruders would depart without incident.

SOUTHSEA CASTLE, PORTSMOUTH

Southsea Castle was built in 1544 and is one of the many forts dotted along the south coast built to defend the shores of merry olde England against a French invasion. Most of the castle's history is concerned with bloodshed and death but the ghost that still walks the confines of this old fortification is not that of a solider killed in a horrific manner as one would expect, but that of a little girl.

In the 1820s a lighthouse was constructed to warn passing and approaching ships of the treacherous and rocky shoreline that awaited them if they did not heed the cautionary tale given to them by the lighthouse. One of the castle's many lighthouse keepers had his family living with him and as with many fathers his young daughter was the apple of his eye.

One day his daughter became ill with scarlet fever, a medical condition that causes a sore throat, bright red tongue and an intense fever. The condition is easily cured in today's technologically advanced society but in the 1800s it was a common cause of death as there were no antibiotics available to treat the symptoms.

After a short time the lighthouse keeper lost his daughter to the ravages of the fever and she died. Since then people have reported seeing the spectre of a young girl moving around the confines of Southsea Castle.

Some claim the ghost is wearing a scarlet coloured dress. Could this be some kind symbolism from the spirit of the young girl to give the eyewitness an idea of what had taken her young life away from her or is it just pure coincidence?

STAR INN, EAST TYTHERLEY, NEAR ROMSEY

This wonderful seventeenth century, quintessentially English country pub, has been the place for a recent, astonishing encounter.

A lady, out with friends and family enjoying a meal at the pub, was making her way back to the main bar, after a brief excursion to the toilets, when she turned and noticed a bare footed woman dressed in what appeared to be a long flowing, white nightgown.

It did not take the lady long to realise the supernatural encounter she was having and her suspicions were further endorsed when the apparition promptly faded from view in front of her very eyes.

Obviously being a public house many a comment will arise along the lines of "how much had she had to drink" but the woman concerned was the designated driver for the evening and being so she remained completely teetotal.

This encounter with the ethereal leftovers of a former person appears, at this stage, to be one of those being in the right place at the right time encounters.

STONEHAM LANE, EASTLEIGH

If you make your way down Stoneham Lane in Eastleigh you will come across the small parish church of St. Nicholas. The church, constructed around 1600, has a modest congregation but is very active with the flock that it does have.

The church has quite an unusual peculiarity about it. Take a good look at the bell tower and you will notice that the clock that adorns its walls only has one hand, the hour hand, so telling the time must prove somewhat difficult!

As with many small parish churches in rural England the church has its integral secret tunnel that allegedly runs from behind the organ to exit somewhere in Stoneham Lane. Years ago a local lady died when a horse and carriage ran over her and killed her instantly. It is the ghost of this woman that has been seen over many years by people living in the area. In fact one of the church's former parish priests said that he could see no reason as to why people's experiences should not be believed, something very unusual for a member of the clergy to announce as their views on ghosts are rather limited.

The ghost is said to take on an unusual colouring and many people comment the ghost is green in appearance. The mortal remains of the lady who now haunts the area are buried in the churchyard and it is said that if you spit on the grave and walk around it three times the ghost then appears to you. Walking anti clockwise around the church also makes a supernatural mist descend upon the cemetery ... can you spot the urban myths within this story?

ST. EDMUND THE MARTYR CHURCH, CROFTON, NEAR GOSPORT

The small village of Crofton, situated between the neighboring villages of Stubbington and Titchfield, has a long history and is mentioned as small districts belonging to the estates at Titchfield in the Domesday Book, a record of the country's lands and estates that was written in 1086.

Nearby Titchfield Abbey was a Presbyterian monastery and it was the monks from Titchfield Abbey that had Saint Edmunds, and the adjoining manor house, built. The shadow of a phantom monk has been reported repeatedly over the years both around the area of the church and also in the manor house.

One guest who was staying at the manor house when it was converted into a hotel even awoke from his slumber to find the ghost sitting on the end of his bed!

ST MARGARET'S CHURCH, EAST WELLOW, NEAR ROMSEY

The twelfth Century church of Saint Margaret of Antioch is a typical English country village church with its dedicated parishioners still cherishing the venue as they have done for hundreds of years.

Probably the most famous of its former worshippers is that of Florence Nightingale, the famed lady with the lamp of the Crimean war. Florence and her family lived near to the church in a sprawling mansion known as Embley Park, which is now a school.

When Florence died on the 13th August 1910, aged 90 years of age, her family was offered a full state burial at Westminster Abbey, as a reflection of the important work that she had done for the medical world. This offer was declined and Florence was interned at St. Margaret's church as she had wanted.

It is claimed that many people have witnessed the wraith of Florence drifting around the graveyard and also entering the church that she loved so dearly.

St. Margaret's Church in East Wellow, near Romsey. The grave of the famed Lady with the Lamp, Florence Nightingale, can be seen to the left in the foreground.

Colonel William Morton, who lived nearby to the church in the seventeenth Century, is also said to haunt the area around the church as does a coach pulled by four horses. The coach is said to run along the small country lanes leading from Embley Park to St. Margaret's every 31st December at midnight. Some witnesses claim that the coach is driverless whilst other have reported seeing a phantom rider urging the horses on.

One of the most recent reports of paranormal phenomena that have occurred at the church within the past few years was experienced by a one Mr. McEwan. Mr. McEwan was inside the church with his wife, taking photos of the various items of interest, when all of a sudden they were treated to a brief burst of choral song. The gentleman was able to distinguish the sound as plainsong and despite his best attempts he was unable to find a rational, logical answer for the experience.

ST. MARY'S CHURCH, ELLINGHAM

St. Mary's Churchyard in Ellingham, near Ringwood, is the final resting place of Dame Alicia Lisle: (see the stories about the Eclipse Inn, Winchester and Moyles Court, Ringwood for more information on Dame Lisle).

On the anniversary of Dame Lisle's horrific death a mysterious red rose is said to appear on her tombstone and no one claims responsibility or seems to know anything about its appearance. Despite staking out the tomb in 2007 I failed to see any red rose appear and after speaking with locals in the area it seems that the red rose has not materialized for many years.

Did the rose fail to appear because I was watching for it, has the person who places it there moved out of the area or subsequently passed away themselves or is this story nothing more than an urban legend. I guess we will never know for sure.

ST. PETER & ST. PAUL'S CHURCH, PORTSMOUTH, HAMPSHIRE

It's a great success when you come across a ghost story where not only the sightings are reliable but also historical information is in the exact same area as where the ghost appears and that is the scenario we have in this instance.

St. Peter and St. Paul's church in Wymering, Portsmouth is a fourteenth century parish church where the ghost of the White Lady, as she is referred to by locals of the area, appears. The white lady is the ghost of Elizabeth Harrison. Elizabeth fell in love with the local land owner's son, only known as Tom, as his surname seems to have dodged history, but her love was not returned. She pursued Tom with diligence, some even say to the point of stalking the man.

One day Elizabeth approached Tom, whilst he was out working in his field, and he promptly turned round and shot Elizabeth dead. Her ghost is often seen wandering through the church graveyard which once was the field where she was shot all those many years ago. Witnesses claim the wraith of poor Elizabeth Harrison wanders the graveyard, occasionally stops, reads a tombstone and then moves on.

What became of Tom, no one knows. There are no records of any trials in the area concerning a man named Tom standing in defence of murder. Is Elizabeth stopping and reading tombstones searching for the grave of her lost love...or is she searching for her own grave?

Elizabeth Harrison' tomb is located just behind a wooden board commemorating the war dead from Cosham and Wymering and her epitaph contains a short poem concerning her death, unfortunately only the first two or three lines of the poem are legible as weathering has taken its toll on the tombstone but you can still read the following lines:

"All friends that this way passeth by, observe the adjacent field, here shot was I."

SWAN INN (FORMERLY THE MUCKY DUCK), PORTSMOUTH

The ghost of a former barmaid is said to haunt the area surrounding the main fireplace in this public house in Guildhall Walk. The barmaid's husband was outraged at his wife for her apparent flouting of their vow to forsake all others and, in a fit of mad jealousy, killed her by the fireplace, some say by using his splicing knife. The murder was apparently witnessed by some of the pub's customers and the sailor was arrested. All my efforts to confirm this story by backing the legend up with historical data has proved fruitless, the last known sighting of the murdered barmaid was by a past landlord's nephew in 1991.

SWORDFISH PUBLIC HOUSE, HILL HEAD, GOSPORT

The Swordfish Pub was located on a spot called Monk's Hill which history tells us was the site of an ancient priory. It has been reported that on warm summer evenings the sound of monastic chanting has been heard drifting around the surrounding area.

It will be interesting to hear if this phenomenon continues as the Swordfish pub has now been demolished to make way for a housing development, will the new residents of these houses encounter the ghostly monks, only time will tell on this one!

TESTWOOD HOUSE, TOTTON

If you're looking for a haunted venue that has a fair collection of ghosts and a disturbing history then Testwood House, in Totton on the outskirts of Southampton, is the place for you. There is a legend, connected to the rambling fifteenth century former hunting lodge, that appears to be an integral part of many haunted house, that of a murder.

It's claimed that a cook was murdered here by a butler, or was it the groom, coachman or manservant? Regardless of who committed the dastardly deed the cook's body was said to have been disposed of across the way from Testwood house in a road that now sports the name of Cook's Lane. Perhaps it is the ghost of the cook that is responsible for the sounds of footsteps coming from the building, particularly strange as the house is fully carpeted and no footfalls of the living can be heard.

There has been a report of a somewhat eerie face peering out of the old pantry window but the most disturbing apparition that occurs at the house is that of the laughing spectre. This ghost, often seen wearing a top hat, a cape and a rather fetching blue and white striped shirt has been seen by numerous people both in the daytime and by those working in the house late at night. A former member of Williams and Humberts staff, a sherry import and export company that once used the building, had a rather disturbing encounter here in January 1965.

The company staff member, a secretary from London, was working late and after he finished his paperwork the secretary decided to leave. Leaving his temporary office, which incidentally occupied the haunted attic which many people claimed, had a foreboding feeling to it, he was rather annoyed to find the house in darkness. Unable to find the lights the gentleman made his way, somewhat precariously, to the front door. When he reached the reception area he was struck by the sight of a male figure dressed in a top hat and cape with his head bent backwards as if in a fit of laughter, laughter which had no sound. The secretary stated he was overcome with sheer and utter fear when he realised what he was witnessing and was extremely relieved when he saw the lights of his taxi coming up the drive to collect him. What makes this story even more interesting is that all the staff members who worked in the house all claimed they had left the lights on and the security guard noted the house was fully lit at eight o clock, half an hour after the scared witless secretary had left.

Who was it that had switched the lights off and then back on again? Was it the laughing ghost subjecting the hapless secretary to a paranormal prank?

THE REGISTRY, PORTSMOUTH

Now the Portsmouth University Students' Union bar this historic building was once the main centre for the registration of Births, Deaths and Marriage in the city.

People in the building late at night, mainly before its conversion to a student bar, claim to have seen a gentlemanly figure dressed in a stove pipe hat and a long grey coat. It is believed this gentleman originates from when the building was once used as a workhouse and its felt that he held some kind of administrative capacity at the workhouse.

THEATRE ROYAL, WINCHESTER

The Theatre Royal, Jewry Street, Winchester, is now a popular destination for people seeking a theatrical merriment but prior to it being a theatre the venue was a hotel called the Market Hotel.

This hotel was converted into the Theatre Royal in 1913 by two brothers, John and James Simpkins and it's the ghost of John Simpkins that still treads the boards of his old theatre to this day.

When the theatre royal was converted from the Market Hotel James Simpkins added a sign above the stage which read "JS". John was somewhat disgruntled over this and insisted the plaque should read "J&JS". James never did fulfill his promise to his brother to have the sign corrected and it is probably because of this oversight that the ghost of John has been seen wandering from the area of his old office, along the circle, and eventually pausing at the one of the theatre's boxes whilst he inspects the sign to note if the correction has yet taken place.

Disappointed at no sign of change the ghost of John then moves off towards the stage and then through a wall where his old office once stood.

The theatre is also home to a crisis apparition. A crisis apparition is the ghost of a living person and their image is somehow thought to project itself across great distances when the person is in extreme distress, pain, close to death or has in fact just died.

During the First World War many of the theatre's male employees were called up for active service to fight in the Great War ... many never returned. During a show one of the actresses looked up and noticed the ghost of a Tommy soldier, she then promptly fainted.

Later the actress was shown a photograph of some former employees who went off to fight and she was able to identify that one of the men in the photographs was indeed the spectre she had sighted during her performance but what makes this story most convincing was that the man's mother had received a telegram notifying her of her son's death the previous day.

Had this young man somehow managed to throw his image back to the theatre, as a crisis apparition, where he had once worked as a spotlight operator or does his wraith haunt the theatre to this day?

TUDOR HOUSE MUSEUM, BUGLE STREET, SOUTHAMPTON

The striking Tudor style building, dominating Saint Michaels Square, which is the Tudor House Museum, is not easily missed by any sightseer visiting the city of Southampton.

The museum began life as three residential properties, circa 1150, but the present building dates from the late fifteenth century and is the former home of Sir Richard Lyster, the Lord Chief Justice of England from 1545 to 1552.

During Sir Lyster's occupancy of the house he paid host to King Henry VIII and Queen Anne Boleyn. It's alleged that the ghost haunting the Tudor House Museum is none other than Anne Boleyn, which is impressive in itself as she also haunts the Tower of London, Blickling Hall in Norfolk and her family home, Hever Castle, in Kent.

Investigators hunting the museum's ghosts have been privy to a host of phenomena including the sound of a bell ringing, footsteps, humanoid shapes and shadows moving about in the rooms being investigated and unexplained scraping noises.

Another of the many places where, allegedly, the ghost of Anne Boleyn still walks to this very day ... the Tudor House Museum in Southampton.

VENTNOR BOTANICAL GARDENS, VENTNOR, ISLE OF WIGHT

The now idyllic layout of the Ventnor Botanical Gardens on the Isle of Wight is a far flung shadow from its previous life as the site of the Royal National Hospital for Diseases of the Chest.

The hospital was established in 1869 and focused its interest on illnesses and diseases that affected the chest, namely tuberculosis. When a treatment was discovered for tuberculosis the hospital's need steadily declined, fell redundant and was then demolished in 1969.

It is the demolition of the hospital that is reported to have rapidly increased the paranormal activity surrounding the location. During the demolition of the operating theatre, which was done by hand as the machinery kept breaking without explanation; workmen started hearing moans, groans and crying. The ghost of a little girl was also spotted on occasion and an electrician at the site had the fright of his life when he spotted a ghostly face peering over the top of the toilet cubicle door he was occupying at the time.

Even to this day people report seeing the ghosts of the hospitals former patients, meandering amongst the plants of the Botanical Gardens and the inexplicable smell of mulled wine, which was made and served to the patients by a former Matron.

Former garden curator, Simon Goodenough, even had a conversation with one of the ghosts. Leaving work late one evening Mr. Goodenough was approached by a gentleman who asked how long he had been at the hospital. Simon replied he had been there for about six months, finished his conversation and left the gardens. On his drive home the words of the man finally hit home. Why did the man ask how long he had been at the hospital when the hospital had not even been there since 1969?

VERNHAM DEAN

During the great plague of 1665 a local parish parson persuaded his flock to take shelter on Conholt Hill with the promise that he would travel to Andover to fetch much needed food and medical supplies.

As the plague ran rampant across England people were reluctant to transfer goods and services to infected villages, towns and cities for fear of becoming infected themselves, so it was up to the parson to bring help or the whole village of Vernham Dean would be condemned to a most terrible fate.

Something went awry in the plan though. The parson never returned as he fell sick by the time he reached the bottom of Conholt Hill. Some suggest that he never intended to return to his flock and instead decided to flee the area and get as far away as possible from the plague ridden villagers. Whether he was planning to flee or did indeed intend to return with food and supplies we will never know for sure, but what we do know is that the spirit of this man still haunts the hillside where he failed his parishioners and perhaps even himself.

WARBLINGTON CASTLE, WARBLINGTON

The former home of the Countess of Salisbury was once a magnificent place, today it is nothing more than a ruin where only one solitary ruined tower still stands.

Margaret, Countess of Salisbury, suffered the indignity of being arrested for opposing Henry VIII during the reformation but the Countess did not go quietly. After her arrest she was subsequently sent to the Tower of London facing charges of treason and when the time for her execution came she ran around the executioner's block saying "These grey hairs know no treason". The executioner pursued her around the scaffolding and eventually, with no manner of professionalism, cut off her head.

Her ghost has been seen wandering around the ruins of her castle and St. Thomas à Becket Church which lays adjacent to her former home. Her wraith has been reported by a whole host of people from everyday walks of life with no thought or concern about ghosts and it seems that the white clad, headless apparition of Margaret will continue to haunt her former home.

WHITE HART HOTEL, ANDOVER

Claiming to be over 300 years old and a venue once frequented by the ousted King Charles I, The White Hart Hotel in Bridge Street, Andover, is home to three spectral patrons.

The hotel's most frequently seen ghost is that of a lady dressed in a dark green cloak. She seems to be particularly attracted to room number 20, as one overnight guest was visited by this spook not once but twice in a single evening, or so it is claimed in Roger Longs *Haunted Inns of Hampshire.*

There have also been reports of two indistinct humanoid figures haunting the ground floor of the hotel. I say indistinct as most eye witness accounts of these ghosts claim they are somewhat transparent and blurry. Many people believe these figures are those of a man and a woman.

Phantom footfalls have also been reported in the White Hart by a maid who stated that the phantom footsteps followed her up the stairs and along a corridor.

White Hart Public House, Cadnam

The small village of Cadnam, a couple of miles away from the Rufus Stone, in the New Forest is a village easily missed.

If you do happen to be in the area, ensure a visit to the White Hart Pub is on your schedule. You won't see the ghost that haunts the pub, in fact I do believe no one ever has, but the spiritual presence of a lady has been detected by other means.

Previous owners have reported the sudden inexplicable smell of perfume and have also reported hearing the sound of silk, swishing along as the ghost walks her haunt. The most bizarre method of discovering if the ghost is around is to keep an eye on a broken clock for the ghostly woman allegedly has the ability to bring back to life clocks that are no longer working.

Got a broken clock? Bring it to the White Hart public house at Cadnam and its resident ghost may well fix it for you!

WHITE HORSE HOTEL, ROMSEY

This hotel, the flagship hotel in the Silks Hotels complex, is one of Romsey's most historical buildings.

Completely renovated and lovingly restored, you cannot help but fall in love with the ambience and appeal of the building with its Tudor wall art, Georgian staircase and fine oak beams.

There has been a building on the site since the ninth century and its connections to Romsey Abbey, as a former lodging house, are intense. The current building dates from the fourteenth century, don't be fooled by its Georgian façade, and part of the hotel, the assembly rooms, is where former Prime Minister Lord Palmerston, first started to publicly debate on the subject of politics.

The White Horse Hotel in Romsey where the ghost of a lady still walks the mummers gallery.

With a rich tapestry of history it is no wonder to discover that the hotel is haunted. A lady in a white dress has been seen to frequent the upper rooms and especially the Mummers Gallery. The gallery was originally open aired and looked down onto the street below.

It is the Mummers Gallery and the area around the Georgian staircase that she has been witnessed the most around, drifting silently through the building.

Who she is, and why she haunts the hotel, no one knows.

WINCHESTER CATHEDRAL, WINCHESTER

The cathedral close is haunted by the ghost of a limping monk but the most interesting of ghostly evidence comes from a photograph taken inside Winchester Cathedral by a tourist in 1957. The photograph shows, what appears to be, thirteen ghostly figures kneeling in prayer at the altar and to my knowledge no rational explanation has yet been offered to explain the photograph.

WYMERING MANOR, PORTSMOUTH

Widely acclaimed as Hampshire's Most Haunted house, this sprawling manor house in the northern suburbs of the city boasts no less than eighteen ghosts although some investigators claim there are more.

Parts of the house, or at least the first house on the site, were constructed after the Norman conquest of 1066 and there is mention of the house in the Doomesday Book of 1086. With a house this steeped in history it's hardly surprising that spectral occurrences are reported on a daily basis. Past owners, residents and visitors to the house have reported laying witness to shadowy figures, face to face encounters with male and female spectres, a baby's crying and the sounds of disembodied voices all reverberate around the property.

One of the most shocking appearances at the house is that of a nun. She stands at the top of a staircase leading to what used to be the servants' rooms in the attic but it is her hands, dripping in blood, that cause shock and alarm. Why her hands are drenched in blood nobody knows but it is rumored, without historical fact to back up the claim I must say, that one of the servant's rooms was once used as a back street abortion clinic in the 1800s. The house has two famous ghosts. The apparition of Sir Francis William Austen, brother of Hampshire author Jane Austen and a former church warden for St. Peter and St. Paul's church which is directly opposite Wymering Manor, has been seen on numerous occasions and has even acknowledged a staff member working at the house with a simple and courteous smile. Sir Francis was also a highly acclaimed officer in the Royal Navy and achieved the rank of Admiral of the fleet.

A further famous ghost at Wymering Manor is that of Sir Roderick of Portchester, otherwise known as Reckless Roddy. It is said that during the medieval period of history a young knight married his bride and rode to Wymering Manor in order to spend their wedding night at the house. The knight was unexpectedly called away to an emergency and left the house. Sir Roderick learned of this news and rode to Wymering Manor in order to seduce the knight's bride. The knight returned, perhaps in the knowledge something was astray, and caught Reckless Roddy in the house. Reckless Roddy fled the scene and tried to mount his steed in the road outside the house, it was the last thing that Roderick would ever do; the knight thrust his sword through Roderick and his body fell to the floor, his horse galloping away at speed.

In 1960 the house was leased by the Youth Hostel Association and the manors first wardens all reported hearing the sound of a horse bolting up the lane outside Wymering Manor at 2 am. Upon investigating the noise they found no horse and were not aware of the legend of Reckless Roddy. Does Sir Roderick's horse still race away from the scene where his master was murdered?

ZIP IMAGESETTERS, ROMSEY

At 33 Church Street, Romsey, lay the offices of Zip Imagesetters, a modern day print and design company whose talents are in demand from many organisations and businesses around the UK.

Despite being adorned with state of the art computers, logos and design work any visitor can easily see and feel the historical nature of the old building. It is from the office's former use, as a shop, which its ghost could well originate from.

I spoke to Michael Windebank about a rather unusual experience he had in the office in 2007. "It was about ten past five on the evening of the 12th July and I had just finished locking the building up and was

Zip Imagesetters in Romsey, where an employee had a most unusual experience.

switching the lights off when I thought I would double check I had everything switched off in the cellar," Michael told me.

"I came through the office and turned to go towards the cellar and there, right in front of me, was what I can only say was a ghost." I was expecting to hear a ghostly story of a phantom man or woman but what Michael told me was something very unusual. "Can you describe the ghost to me?" I enquired. "Yeah, it was just a pale blue dress, no arms, no legs, no head. In fact there was no appearance of a body at all wearing the dress." Historical research into the building's previous occupants revealed that one former resident was in fact a dress maker!

As soon as he had witnessed the phantom dress it appeared to turn on the spot and vanish into thin air. Pressing Mr. Windebank for further details he went on to to tell me that the ghost was roughly five foot in height, semi transparent and also self illuminated as the lights were off but it was still clearly visible.

Michael Windebank on the stairs of Zip Imagesetters where he witnessed a ghostly dress.

BIBLIOGRAPHY

Baldwin, Gay, *Isle of Wight Ghosts: Book Four* (1999)
Brode, Anthony, *Haunted Hampshire* (1981)
Brooks, John, *The Good Ghost Guide* (1994)
Burbridge, Spinney & Genge, *Romsey – A photographic history of your town* (2005)
Fox, Ian, *The Haunted Places of Hampshire* (2000)
Hampshire Ghost Club, *Investigation Archives* (2001-2008)
Harries, John, *The Ghost Hunters Road Book* (1968)
Holland, Alec, *Bucklers Hard: A Rural Shipbuilding Centre* (1985)
Lewis, Roy Harley, *Theatre Ghosts* (1988)
Long, Roger, *Haunted Inns of Hampshire* (1999)
Millson, Cecilia, *Tales of Old Hampshire* (1980)
Montagu, Elizabeth, *Honorable Rebel* (2003)
Montagu, Lord, *Wheels within Wheels* (2000)
Parr, Donald, *Web of Fear* (1996)
Puttick, Betty, *Supernatural England* (2002)
Rogers, Peter, *Wymering Manor – Outline Historical Notes* (privately published book)
Ross, Patricia, *Hampshire Hauntings & Hearsay* (1998)
Sutherland, Jonathan, *Ghosts of Great Britain* (2001)
Southgate, Michael, *The Old Tide Mill at Eling*
Underwood, Peter, *A-Z of British Ghosts* (1971)
Underwood, Peter, *Guide to Ghosts and Haunted Places* (1999)
Underwood, Peter, *Nights in Haunted Houses* (1994)

ABOUT THE AUTHOR

The author's interest in the paranormal started in 1986 when his sister moved into a three bedroom council house in the northern suburbs of Portsmouth. Shortly after moving into the property all kinds of supernatural activity started which included objects being thrown around, black shadowy figures seen flitting up and down the stairs and the spectre of a man wearing 1940s clothing seen standing in the back garden of the house. It was this poltergeist ridden house that started David on the path he now treks.

In 2001 David established the Hampshire Ghost Club whose aims were, and still are to this very day, to investigate claims of paranormal phenomena and where possible record this evidence for dissemination amongst the public at large. The Hampshire Ghost Club gained a high reputation quickly and still stands out as a major 'Ghost Hunting' society investigating all sorts of locations around the UK but specializing in hauntings of the county of Hampshire. David and the Hampshire Ghost Club's high reputation have meant they have been consulted on cases for the Royal Navy, County Councils and even a member of the British Aristocracy.

Over the years the author has collected a plethora of stories concerning the ghosts that haunt Hampshire and after so many years of researching and investigated ghosts and haunted places this book is the result of the many stories and legends he has encountered, and in many circumstances, investigated personally.

The public have seen David's work in action with numerous Radio and TV appearances including Living TV's popular series Most Haunted.

David was born in Portsmouth, Hampshire, and currently resides in the small market town of Romsey with his wife and three children.